The humongous

book of
Bible Skits

for children's ministry

Group
Loveland, Colorado

Group resources actually work!

This Group resource helps you focus on **"The 1 Thing"™**—a life-changing relationship with Jesus Christ. "The 1 Thing" incorporates our **R.E.A.L.** approach to ministry. It reinforces a growing friendship with Jesus, encourages long-term learning, and results in life transformation, because it's:

Relational
Learner-to-learner interaction enhances learning and builds Christian friendships.

Experiential
What learners experience through discussion and action sticks with them up to 9 times longer than what they simply hear or read.

Applicable
The aim of Christian education is to equip learners to be both hearers and doers of God's Word.

Learner-based
Learners understand and retain more when the learning process takes into consideration how they learn best.

The Humongous Book of Bible Skits for Children's Ministry
Copyright © 2006 Group Publishing, Inc.

Visit our Web site: **www.group.com**

Credits
Authors: Teryl Cartwright, John R. Cutshall, Ruthie Daniels, Enelle G. Eder, Lynda Freeman, Jan Kershner, Scott M. Kinner, Larry Shallenberger, Faye Spieker, and April Thoms
Editors: Roxanne Wieman and Mikal Keefer
Chief Creative Officer: Joani Schultz
Copy Editor: Dena Twinem
Art Directors: Jean Bruns (interior) and Josh Emrich (cover)
Assistant Art Director: Joyce Douglas
Book Designer: Boven Design Studio
Illustrator: Amy Wummer
Print Production Artist: Pat Reinheimer
Production Manager: Peggy Naylor

Unless otherwise noted, Scripture taken from the HOLY BIBLE, NEW INTERNATIONAL VERSION®. Copyright © 1973, 1978, 1984 by International Bible Society. Used by permission of Zondervan Publishing House. All rights reserved.

Library of Congress Cataloging-in-Publication Data
The humongous book of Bible skits for children's ministry.
      p.   cm.
      Includes indexes.
ISBN 0-7644-3083-1 (pbk. : alk. paper)
1. Religious drama, American. 2. Bible--History of Biblical events--Juvenile drama. 3. Children's plays, American. 4. Bible plays, American. I. Group Publishing.
PS627.R4H86 2006
268'.432--dc22   2005023773

Printed in the United States of America.
10 9 8 7 6 5 4   15 14 13 12 11 10 09 08 07 06

Contents

◆ *Here's how to super-size the fun and learning from your skits*

✫ ✫ ✫ ✫ ✫

THE SKITS
*Use these no-prep skits to get every student involved—
and make Bible Stories come alive!*

✫ ✫ ✫ ✫ ✫

☆ ☆ ☆ ☆ ☆
INDEXES
☆ ☆ ☆ ☆ ☆

Introduction

Congratulations!

You now have at your fingertips 52 fun, easy-to-use Bible skits. Use them to spice up a lesson, fill an extra few minutes at the end of class, or as a weekly lesson-launcher—for an entire year!

These skits don't require costumes, rehearsals, or elaborate props. If you've got a room full of kids and an open area to use as a stage, you have everything necessary to pull off a skit on short notice.

But maybe you're new to using drama in your children's ministry. You're wondering how to guarantee that each skit will be kid-pleasing...memorable...and will make for solid Bible learning.

Here's some practical advice for getting the most from each and every skit...

Keep the first thing first.

What exactly is the "first thing"?

Hint: It's *not* the quality of your performance.

There's no Oscar awarded in the category of "Best Children's Ministry Skit." You and your kids are under no pressure to put on a flawless production.

So relax...and focus instead on getting every child involved in each skit. Because while the quality of the production isn't critical, the quality of the *learning* is, and involved children learn more and retain what they learn longer.

Use the debriefing questions provided at the end of each skit, and you'll engage children even more completely. You'll cement the learning even firmer in kids' minds and hearts.

Play the role of Narrator yourself.

The Narrator is an important role. The Narrator has the most difficult lines, directs the action, sets the pace, and acts as a prompter. If you're acting as the Narrator, you'll be able to manage the flow of the skit.

Make it safe for children to be in the skits.

Some children take to the stage like ducks to water. They *love* having the spotlight turned their direction. They're natural-born thespians.

But other children become anxious when asked to speak in front of a crowd... and in their minds, "crowd" means two or more people. For shy children, the notion of being in a skit inspires terror.

It's your job to make certain that participating in skits is a positive, safe experience for everyone. Here are three ways to meet that goal:

◆ **Be sensitive to reading skills.** Children with speaking roles will read their lines aloud. Don't place children with shaky reading skills in roles that have a lot of lines unless you give them a chance to prepare ahead of time.

◆ **Don't pressure children into roles.** It's easy for us to think cajoling children into activities is doing them a favor. We figure once children jump in, they'll enjoy themselves.

But that may not be true at all. If a child is uncomfortable in a speaking role, cast that child in a nonspeaking, group role. If a child is uncomfortable with even *that*, give the child the role of prompter, Flipper of the Light Switch, or any other off-stage role you can create.

But at all costs, *get every child involved in some way*. In these skits, there's no such thing as an audience—only participants!

◆ **Be affirming—and don't allow criticism.** Maybe Jerry stumbled over his lines or missed a cue—so what? Who cares? You set the tone when it comes to generating applause and overlooking blunders, so be deliberately gracious.

Don't sweat the stage.

In a perfect world, you have a large elevated area at one end of your room. It's lit professionally, and the sound technician takes care of all the microphones.

Don't live in that world? Neither do most people.

All you need is an open area so kids can move around easily. And depending on the number of children in your ministry, you don't even need a *large* area.

The fun isn't in the staging, props, and costumes. It's in getting kids involved and learning!

Do sweat the staging.

Each skit provides a quick description about where kids are standing when the skit starts and provides information about moving around the stage. It's worth noting these instructions because they let children move in logical ways through the skit.

Just in case you're not familiar with stage directions, here's a cheat sheet for your use.

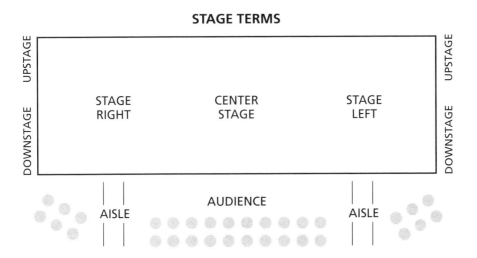

Use the CD to make skits come alive.

Each skit comes with a specific sound effect that helps set the stage for your skit. Sometimes it's a background sound you'll play nonstop throughout the skit. Other times it's a very specific sound you'll use to highlight an element of the narrative.

Place your CD player where you can easily reach it, and adjust the sound before the skit begins.

Finally—have fun!

Kids take their cues—literally and emotionally—from you. If you're having fun, your kids will, too.

So have a blast with these skits...and enjoy leading your kids into a deeper understanding of 52 must-know Bible events!

A Word About Photocopying Scripts and CDs

Feel free to make as many copies of scripts as you desire for use in your own church's ministries. You have complete permission to do so, whether you need two scripts or 200.

And a suggestion: When you photocopy scripts for your children, hit the "enlarge" button on your copier. The larger print will be easier for some children to read. We enlarged pages 20% and the script pages easily fit on an 8½x11-inch sheet.

The CD *can't* be legally reproduced, however. Use it in your ministry, but please don't burn additional copies.

Thanks for demonstrating integrity to the children you serve in how you use this ministry resource.

Lions and Tigers and Trees-- Oh, My!

The Scene: a garden

The Simple Setup: You'll need no furniture on the stage; an open area where it's easy for your "animals" to move around is best.

For Extra Impact: Consider giving children playing the role of Trees green pieces of paper to use as leaves.

Bible Story
Adam and Eve

Scripture
Genesis 2:4-25

The Characters

Narrator: a friendly storyteller

Adam: a guy

Eve: a girl

Trees: kids willing to hold their hands over their heads and "twinkle" their fingers

Animals: kids who'll impersonate animals mentioned

The Skit

After you've assigned the roles of Adam and Eve, form the rest of your children into two groups: the Trees and the Animals. If you have just a few children, let them play both roles.

As the skit begins, the stage is empty. Narrator may be offstage or at one side of the stage throughout the skit.

Start the "Adam and Eve" track on *The Humongous Book of Bible Skits for Children's Ministry* CD (track 1). Set your CD player on "repeat" so the track repeats.

Narrator: This is the account of the heavens and the earth when they were created. After God created the earth, he planted a garden in the east, in Eden. That's where he put the MAN he formed.

Adam: I think I'll go EAST. Which direction IS that, I wonder.

Narrator: The man went to where the GARDEN was planted. The garden was full of beautiful TREES. Plus, the trees were loaded with FRUIT the man could be pluck and eat. The trees had branches that reached high into the air. The trees' leaves fluttered softly in the breeze and gave the man cool shade.

The man—whose name was ADAM—loved living in the garden.

God told the man that there was just ONE TREE whose fruit Adam couldn't eat. It was the tree of the knowledge of good and evil. Adam sometimes looked at the tree.

Adam: You know, that's a really nice tree. And the fruit on the tree looks wonderful. But if God doesn't want me to eat that fruit, I guess I'll have to find something else for breakfast.

Narrator: Adam didn't have any trouble finding food in the garden. For breakfast he harvested something he called EARFRUIT. He reached high into trees and gently pulled off ears of the dangly fruit.

Adam: Yum! This ear is great! And when I EAT earfruit, my hearing gets better!

Narrator: For lunch Adam ate NOSEPLANT.

Adam: Yum! This nose is tasty! And it SMELLS so good! One just isn't enough. I'm going to pick some MORE noses!

Narrator: Yuck! For dinner Adam ate FINGER food.

Adam: These are GREAT!

Narrator: For Adam, living in the garden was just like living in a restaurant. He could eat good things all day, every day. And because it was his job to care for the garden, he planted just the vegetables he liked.

Adam: No eggplants in MY garden!

Narrator: God formed out of the ground all the beasts of the field and all the birds of the air.

Adam: Look at all those flying things! So THEY'RE what I've heard singing in the trees. I wonder what they're called?

Narrator: God brought the animals to ADAM to see what Adam would name them.

Adam: Look at THAT animal! It walks on four legs. It makes a growling sound. It has big, pointy teeth. I think I'll name it an four-leg-growly-big-teethy. Or maybe I'll call it a lion.

And look at THAT animal! It's very little. It has squinty eyes. It has whiskers that shake when it moves its nose. That must be a mole.

And what's up with THAT animal? It has feet like a kangaroo…a pouch like a kangaroo…it jumps like a kangaroo. Wait—I get it! It's a KANGAROO!

Narrator: It takes a very long time to name all the animals when you start with aardvarks and have to get all the way to zebras. Adam was tired, so he lay down on the ground and went to sleep.

God looked at Adam and knew that Adam needed a helper. He needed someone who was like him, but different.

While Adam was asleep, God took one of Adam's ribs out of his body.

Adam: OW! That HURT!

Narrator: God used the rib to make a woman. Her name was EVE. She was different from the other animals. For starters, she stood on two feet. She had thumbs that worked—just look at her give the "thumbs up" sign. She didn't have fur on her face, and she didn't breathe through gills. Eve was a PERSON, not just another animal. She was waiting for ADAM to wake up, but Adam kept sleeping.

Adam kept SNORING.

Eve finally called his name, but he didn't wake up.

Eve: Adam, wake up. Adam, it's time to get up. Adam? Adam? ADAM, GET UP OR YOU DON'T GET ANY PANCAKES!

Narrator: THAT woke him up! He jumped to his feet, rubbed his eyes, and looked confused.

Adam: Who are you? WHAT are you? And why does my side hurt?

Eve: I'm Eve, and I'm living here in the garden now, too. I'm a person, like you.

Adam:	Are you going to help with the garden?
Eve:	Sure.
Adam:	Are you going to help with the animals?
Eve:	It looks like you could USE some help. There are so MANY of them.
Adam:	I think I'm going to call you "woman" because you were taken out of me and I'm a man. And WHAT was that you said about pancakes?
Narrator:	And so Adam and Eve lived in the garden together…and it was good.

To Talk About

◆ Adam may have been lonely before Eve arrived. Describe a time you were lonely—how did it feel? What helped you feel better?

◆ God provided Adam a companion and met Adam's need for friendship. In what ways has God provided friendships for you?

◆ God gave Adam work to do in the garden. In what ways do you think having work to do is a good thing? a challenge? What sort of work do you enjoy doing?

Topical Tie-Ins: Friendships, Loneliness, Work

Two Brothers, Two Gifts

The Scene: a field

The Simple Setup: You'll need no furniture on stage; an open area works well.

For Extra Impact: Consider giving the Stalks of Grain green sheets of paper to wave in the air as leaves. You could also let the Sheep make and wear construction paper ears covered with cotton balls.

Bible Story
Cain and Abel

Scripture
Genesis 4:1-16

The Characters

Narrator: a friendly storyteller

Cain: a guy

Abel: a guy

God: a child able to speak in a loud, deep voice

Sheep: kids willing to crawl and bleat like sheep

Stalks of Grain: kids willing to wave their arms in the air like stalks of grain in the wind

The Skit

After you've assigned the roles of Cain, Abel, and God, form the rest of your children into two groups: the Sheep and the Stalks of Grain.

As the skit begins, the stage is empty. God should remain offstage throughout the skit, with only his voice audible. Narrator may be offstage or at one side of the stage throughout the skit.

 Start the "Cain and Abel" track on *The Humongous Book of Bible Skits for Children's Ministry* CD (track 2). Set your CD player on "repeat" so the track repeats.

Narrator: Adam and Eve had two sons. One was named CAIN and one was named ABEL. Here they come now. Take a bow, boys. When they grew up, Abel became a SHEPHERD who cared for sheep.

Abel: Come here, little sheep. Come this way. I have some food for you. My, you're noisy today, with all that bleating and baa-ing. You must be hungry! You're great sheep, you know that? I LOVE taking care of you.

Narrator: When Cain grew up, he became a FARMER.

Cain: Plant and sow, water each row, this is the way my stalks of grain grow. Just look at those stalks of grain, standing tall and proud, waving gently in the breeze. They bend left. They bend right. They bend forward and now backward. They're perfect!

Narrator: When it was time for the harvest, Cain presented some of his crops as a GIFT for God.

Cain: Hmm. I wonder which stalks of grain I should give to God. They ALL look good, but some do look better than others. Those on this side of the field look tastiest, and I'd like to eat those myself. Those other stalks are pretty good. I think I'll give THOSE to God.

Narrator: So Cain cut some of the pretty good stalks of grain and carried them to the ALTAR. He presented them to God.

Abel also brought a gift for God—some SHEEP from his flock.

Abel: Hmm. I wonder which sheep I should give to God. They ALL look good, grazing in the field. See how fluffy their wool is? See how they smile big sheepy smiles? They're all beautiful, but some ARE fluffier than others. Those sheep over there look OK—but not good enough for God! I want to give God the very BEST, the firstborn sheep of my flock!

Narrator: So ABEL chose the very BEST sheep from his flock—the fluffiest and smiliest—and presented them to God. God accepted Abel and his gift, but God DIDN'T accept Cain and his gift. Cain got angry and stomped his feet. He crossed his arms and frowned.

God: Why are you angry, Cain? If you do what's right, you'll be accepted. But if you REFUSE to do what's right, watch out! Sin is just waiting for you, wanting to control you. So YOU have to be in control, not sin.

Narrator: Cain looked like he was listening to God, but INSIDE he was still angry. He clenched his jaw and opened and shut his fists. He was still really mad! And he STAYED mad!

Then one day, Cain had an IDEA. He rubbed his hands together and laughed to himself. Then he called out to his brother.

Cain: Hey, Abel, I've got a GREAT idea. Let's go out into my fields together, OK?

Abel: Uh, OK, I guess. But why?

Cain: Oh, no reason, Let's just spend some time together.

Narrator: So Abel shrugged his shoulders and agreed. The two brothers walked off to the fields together. While they were there, Cain ATTACKED Abel. Cain KILLED his brother! Then Cain walked back home. God had a few questions for Cain.

God: Cain, where is your brother? Where is Abel?

Cain: How should I know? Am I my brother's keeper?

Narrator: God wasn't fooled by Cain's shrug and questions. And God wasn't happy with Cain.

God: Cain, I KNOW what you did. Now you'll be punished! I'm sending you away. And no matter how hard you work, now your crops won't grow. You're going to be homeless. You'll wander the earth!

Narrator: So Cain packed his things, and trudged off alone, through the fields. The sheep cried softly because they missed their shepherd, Abel. The stalks of grain drooped and wilted. And Cain settled far away, east of Eden.

To Talk About

◆ Abel gave God the very best of his sheep to honor God. What can you do that shows God you honor him?

◆ God warned Cain not to let sin control him. What sin have you struggled with in the past?

◆ Cain's punishment was being sent away from God. Thankfully, because of Jesus, we can have forgiveness for our sins and be close to God. How does that make you feel?

Topical Tie-Ins: Obedience, Honoring God, Sin, Anger

The World Takes a Bath

Bible Story
Noah's Flood

Scripture
Genesis 6:5–7:12

The Scene: God is in heaven looking at the earth below.
The Simple Setup: You'll need a chair at center stage. Also, give the weatherman a small umbrella to use as a microphone and then to open when he talks about rain.
For Extra Impact: Consider using simple costumes: a beard for God and a small toy boat for Noah.

The Characters

Narrator: a friendly storyteller
God: a child who can speak with a deep voice
Noah: a guy

Weatherman: a TV-type personality
Animals: kids willing to impersonate animals as those animals are mentioned

The Skit

After you've assigned the roles of God, Noah, and the Weatherman, give the rest of your children roles as Animals.

Place Noah and God at center stage. God sits in a chair, and Noah is on the ground in front of God, facing away from him. The Narrator is at the side of the stage. Place the Animals near center stage.

Narrator: God knew what was happening on earth, and he wasn't pleased.

God: *(Sounding worried and shaking his head)* I don't like that. Nope, I don't like that either. As a matter of fact THAT is really bad. And that over there is really, REALLY BAD!

Narrator: The more God watched, the worse things looked. And the worse things looked, the SADDER God became.

God: Wow. That isn't how I wanted people to treat each other. These people are just flat-out WICKED. I'm sorry I ever MADE them! The only person who's following me is THAT guy over there—Noah!

Noah: *(Turns to God, startled.)* Did I hear my name?

Narrator: God told Noah that he had a job for Noah to do. It was a BIG job, so Noah paid careful attention.

God: I want you and your sons to build a boat. It's called an ark. The ark needs to be 450 feet long, 75 feet wide, and 45 feet high. Build three floors in it, but only ONE door.

Narrator: God told Noah to make the boat out of a certain kind of wood. It had to have rooms on all three floors. And the boat had to keep out water.

Noah: That last part sounds like a GREAT idea. But what happens after I finish the ark?

God: Then you'll fill the ark with animals. I'm going to flood the earth and only you, your family, and the animals on the ark will live. Every OTHER animal and person will die in the flood.

Noah: I'm REALLY glad you asked me to build this ark, God! I'll get busy right away!

Narrator: Noah built the ark just as God instructed. When the ark was ready, all the animals came in right on schedule.

Noah: (*Directing the other students like an orchestra*) Look! There are some elephants! (*Pause for students to impersonate animals.*) There are sheep! (*Pause.*) And there are parrots and penguins! (*Pause.*) Hey, look at the mosquitoes! (*Pause.*)

Narrator: After the animals and Noah's family entered the ark, God closed the door.

 Start the "Noah" track on *The Humongous Book of Bible Skits for Children's Ministry* **CD (track 3). Set your CD player on "repeat" so the track repeats.**

Weatherman: (*Holds closed umbrella as a microphone.*) I'm the weatherman, and I'm here to tell you, it's a beautiful day! The sun is out and there's not a cloud…WAIT a minute…there IS a cloud in the sky. And another one and another one! And they're LEAKING! (*Holds the open umbrella over his head and speaks into the handle.*) It's a sloppy, nasty mess out there. Puddles are turning into ponds. Ponds are turning into lakes. It's a suddenly soggy situation!

Narrator: God kept his promise. It rained for 40 days and nights as the earth flooded and the ark floated. On the ark, the animals leaned to the left when waves came from the right. They leaned to the right when waves came from the left. And when waves came from both directions, they stayed in one place and jiggled! God kept everyone and everything in the ark safe—which is a VERY happy ending!

 # To Talk About

◆ God saved Noah and his family because they were friends of God and lived like God wanted them to live. In what ways do you live for God?

◆ In what ways can you grow in your friendship with God?

Topical Tie-Ins: Obedience, Family, Sin

The Babblin' Bunch

The Scene: a construction site

The Simple Setup: The stage should be open, with room in the background to begin assembling a tower. For props provide a selection of tape measures, toy hammers, and other safe tools for the builders to carry.

For Extra Impact: Make large building blocks by stuffing a grocery bag with newspaper. Then slide another bag over the top and tape around the bottom.

Bible Story
The Tower of Babel

Scripture
Genesis 11:1-9

The Characters

Narrator: a friendly storyteller

Carlos: boy

Fritz: boy

Pierre: boy

Lilly: girl

Carpenters & Workers: children willing to carry tools and small pieces of wood across stage as they pretend to work on the tower

Sound Person: a nonspeaking role for a child who will turn the CD on and off at appropriate times

The Skit

As the skit begins, the three boys are at center stage, talking. Carpenters and Workers are offstage. Narrator is offstage or at one side of the stage.

Narrator: After the great flood, when God spared Noah and his family, the world needed to fill with people again. Noah's kids had kids, and then THEIR kids had kids, and then their kids' kids had kids, and…Well you get the picture. All these people started spreading out over the land. And everyone on the earth spoke the same LANGUAGE.

Carlos: Morning, Fritz, Morning Pierre. BEAUTIFUL day isn't it?

Fritz: Sure is. The sky is so clear I bet you can see for miles!

Pierre: Yeah! Miles and miles—straight up! *(Looks up and points.)*

Carlos: You know, I've been thinking lately.

Fritz: I THOUGHT I heard something squeaking!

Pierre:	Me too, but I figured Hiram's donkey cart was stuck in the mud again!
Carlos:	Just listen. Wouldn't it be AWESOME to build ourselves a tower that could reach up to the HEAVENS?
Fritz:	I think he's serious!
Pierre:	It WOULD be cool! If we had a tower like that, people would think we were really important. But what would we MAKE it out of?
Carlos:	Easy—we could make BRICKS and bake the bricks in the sun until they got hard.
Fritz:	WAY cool! A BRICK tower!
Pierre:	If we had a tower like THAT, people would really look UP to us! Get it guys? LOOK UP to us!
	(The three boys exit stage left.)
Narrator:	The more people talked about it, the more they wanted to build the tower. Pretty soon, lots of Carpenters and Workers were busy working on the tower.
	(Carpenters and workers enter and start measuring and building in the background as the boys return. Lilly follows, carrying a bucket and cup.)

Start the "Tower of Babel" track on *The Humongous Book of Bible Skits for Children's Ministry* CD (track 4). Set your CD player on "repeat" so the track repeats.

Fritz:	*(Calls to workers.)* Looking good! Keep up the good WORK!
Lilly:	Hi guys! Anybody like a drink of water? It is really hot out here today!
Carlos:	Thanks! I've worked up a sweat and it isn't even noon yet!
Pierre:	Same here! I wasn't meant for MANUAL LABOR.
Fritz:	But just think: OUR OWN TOWER. It'll reach as high as GOD. We'll be ENVIED by the whole world! Think of all the POWER we'll have.
	(All four children exit.)

Narrator: The higher the tower grew, the PROUDER the people became of THEIR accomplishment. They were PLEASED, but GOD wasn't. God said, "If speaking ONE LANGUAGE makes it possible for them to do this, I'll stop their project by CONFUSING their language. Then they'll see they must depend on me, not on themselves!"

(Lilly and the three boys return to the stage.)

Lilly: Good morning guys. Can I get you some water?

Fritz: DANKE. *(pronounced* "dawnk-uh"*)*

Lilly: Huh? What did you say?

Fritz: DANKE!

Lilly: Whatever. I'll just give Carlos a drink since you don't want to talk with me. *(Turns to Carlos.)* Do you want a drink of water?

Carlos: ¡Muchas Gracias! *(pronounced* "moo-chus gra-see-us"*)*

Lilly: OK, what's going on here? Do you or don't you want some water?

Carlos: ¡Si, muchas gracias!

Lilly: *(Getting frustrated)* This isn't funny, guys! Pierre, would YOU like to have a drink of water?

Pierre: MERCI BEAUCOUP. *(pronounced* "mare-see bo-coo"*)*

Lilly: Oh, no! You're in on this, too! If you three are going to talk so GOOFY, I'll just let you be thirsty. I'm out of here! *(Lilly exits in a huff stage right.)*

Narrator: The confusion didn't stop. See how the workers are looking at each other and looking CONFUSED? They're shaking their heads. They're shrugging. When they talk they can't understand each other! That means they can't WORK together, either.

Turn off track 4.

Narrator: All the work on the tower came to a stop. People who could understand each other formed groups and scattered all over the world. The great TOWER was never finished. In time it was called THE TOWER OF BABEL, which means "The LORD CONFUSED the LANGUAGE."

To Talk About

◆ The people wanted to build a tower. Was it wrong to build something? How did what they were doing *become* wrong? How did their attitudes change as the tower grew taller?

◆ Have you ever met someone who spoke a different language from you? What part of the world was this person from? How did you communicate?

◆ God was angry when he saw the tower. Why do you think God wasn't pleased with their project? Can people have more power than God? Why or why not?

Topical Tie-Ins: Power, Communication, Work, Cooperation

Joseph and His Many Brothers

The Scene: wheat field

The Simple Setup: You'll need no furniture on the stage, but a few plants can suggest the outdoors; you'll need a large open area for the action.

For Extra Impact: Give Joseph a colorful coat.

Bible Story
Joseph and His Brothers

Scripture
Genesis 37:1-36

The Characters

Narrator: a spunky storyteller

Joseph: a guy with a cocky attitude

Brothers: up to 11 guys or girls with attitude, wearing baseball caps

Camels: one or more children who'll crawl on all fours and make a spitting sound

Traders: one or more children who'll *gently* lead Joseph away

The Skit

Choose a good reader for the role of Joseph and outgoing kids to be Brothers. If you have a small class, you may use fewer than 11 Brothers and include girls as Brothers. Allow Brothers to practice their chants offstage. Coach Traders to "ride" the Camels by having the Camels crawl on all fours while the Traders walk carefully astride them.

As the skit begins, the stage is empty, except for a few plants. Narrator stands stage right throughout the skit. Joseph is center stage.

Start the "Joseph and His Brothers" track on *The Humongous Book of Bible Skits for Children's Ministry* CD (track 5). Set your CD player on "repeat" so the track repeats.

Narrator: Joseph was a guy…

Joseph: A COOL guy!

Narrator: Sorry. Joseph was a COOL guy who had 11 brothers.

Joseph: Oh no! ELEVEN brothers! I think I'm in trouble here! That's 11 guys to give me a hard time!

Brothers: (Chanting) We're BIG! We're BAD! We're BIG, BAD BROTHERS!

Joseph: That's 11 brothers to hide my stuff!

Brothers: (Chanting) We're BIG! We're BAD! We're BIG, BAD BROTHERS!

Joseph: That's 11 brothers to…

Narrator: Can we get on with the STORY here?

Joseph: Sorry.

Brothers: Sorry.

Narrator: The 12 brothers were the sons of Jacob. To tell you the truth, Jacob liked Joseph the best.

Joseph: COOL!

Brothers: Grrrr!

Joseph: Sorry!

Narrator: Jacob made Joseph a brightly colored coat.

Brothers: (Chanting) We want a COAT! We want a COAT! We want a COAT!

Narrator: ENOUGH!

Brothers: Sorry!

Narrator: One night, Joseph had a dream. He told his brothers about it.

Joseph: Hey, big, bad brothers! I had a dream that we were in the field making bundles of WHEAT. Then, all of a sudden, MY bundle of wheat stood up and all your bundles of wheat bowed down to it. Cool, huh?

Brothers: Grrrr!

Joseph: Sorry!

Narrator: The brothers didn't think Joseph's dream was so cool. They were angry and jealous. See how they're stomping around and how they have on grumpy faces? Then Joseph had ANOTHER dream. This time he dreamed that the SUN, MOON, and 11 STARS bowed down to him.

Brothers: Grrrr!

Joseph: Sorry!

Narrator: Joseph's brothers were VERY angry. The brothers decided to get even with Joseph.

Brothers: We're BIG! We're BAD! We're BIG, BAD BROTHERS!

Narrator: They decided to kill Joseph!

Joseph: NOW WAIT JUST A MINUTE! I get KILLED in this story? Nobody told me I was going to get KILLED!

Narrator: Don't worry, you don't get killed.

Joseph: That's better!

Narrator: You just get thrown in a well and left to die!

Joseph: WHAT?

Narrator: I can't hear you Joseph. You're in a well. Quiet down and let me get on with the story. Joseph's brother, Reuben, didn't want to kill Joseph, so he talked the other Big Bad Brothers into throwing Joseph down a well. Reuben planned to come back later to rescue Joseph.

Joseph: THAT'S more like it!

Narrator: But before Reuben could rescue Joseph, some CAMELS came along. Camels aren't very nice creatures. They spit a lot and it sounds like a big popping "P" sound. The CAMELS were POPPING and CLOP-PING along, carrying TRADERS. The BROTHERS sold Joseph to the TRADERS for 20 PIECES OF SILVER.

Joseph: Hey! THAT'S all I'm worth?

Narrator: Shh. You're in slavery now. Go with the traders and watch out for the camels. They spit. The brothers spilled animal blood on Joseph's coat and showed the coat to their father. The brothers told Jacob that Joseph had been eaten by a wild animal. Jacob was very sad.

Joseph: That's it? I've been sold into SLAVERY? My father thinks I'm DEAD? That can't be the END of the story!

Narrator: It isn't.

Joseph: I KNEW it! I get rescued and get even with my BROTHERS, right?

Narrator: Not exactly.

Brothers: Sorry! But not really!

Joseph: So I get rescued and become a famous music star and have my own tour and television show and everything?

Narrator: Not exactly.

Brothers: Sorry! But STILL not really!

Joseph: Well, what DOES happen?

Narrator: You become a servant in an Egyptian household…but God isn't through with you yet!

 ## To Talk About

◆ How do you think Joseph felt when his brothers betrayed him? After what his brothers did to him, do you think Joseph trusted them? Why or why not?

◆ Have people ever been mean to you? How did you handle it?

◆ How can God help us when we're sad? How can we help others who might be feeling that way?

Topical Tie-Ins: Loneliness, Friendship, Fear, Trust

Sweet Dreams

The Scene: Pharaoh's palace

The Simple Setup: You'll need two chairs placed at center stage and an open area on either side of the chairs. One chair will be Pharaoh's throne.

For Extra Impact: Drape a sheet over Pharaoh's chair so it looks like a throne. Give the wise men of Egypt clipboards, pencils, and books so they can pretend to be studying the problem and looking for answers.

Bible Story
Joseph Interprets
Pharaoh's Dreams

Scripture
Genesis 41:1-40

The Characters

Narrator: a friendly storyteller

Pharaoh: a guy

Joseph: another guy

Wise Men of Egypt: a mixed crowd

Cupbearer: a guy or a girl

Cows: kids who will pretend to be cows

Heads of Grain: kids who will pretend to be heads of grain

The Skit

After you've assigned the roles of Pharaoh, Joseph, and the Cupbearer, form the rest of your children into three groups: cows in Pharaoh's dream, stalks of grain, and the wise men of Egypt. If you have lots of kids, form separate groups for the fat and skinny cows, and healthy and sickly grain. If you have a few children, ask kids to play more than one role.

As the skit begins, the stage is empty except for Pharaoh, who appears to be sleeping on his throne. Pharaoh is snoring. Narrator may be offstage or at one side of the stage throughout the skit.

Narrator: PHARAOH was the leader of Egypt, but that didn't keep him from having some weird dreams. One time he dreamed he saw seven healthy, fat cows come up out of the river and begin eating grass. Boy, were they hungry! They ate and they ATE. See them gobble grass? Then Pharaoh dreamed that seven sickly, SKINNY cows come to stand by the fat cows. The SKINNY cows ate the FAT COWS. Pharaoh woke up in a hurry!

Pharaoh: Whoa, what a DREAM! Totally DISGUSTING! At least it was just a dream. I need some beauty sleep—a pharaoh's gotta look good, you know.

Narrator: So Pharaoh fell asleep again. See him dozing off? This time he dreamed that he saw seven plump, healthy HEADS OF GRAIN growing on one stalk. See the grain waving in the breeze? Then seven shriveled, skinny heads of grain appeared. And then…you guessed it…the skinny heads of grain ATE the fat heads of grain!

Start the "Joseph Interprets Pharaoh's Dreams" track on *The Humongous Book of Bible Skits for Children's Ministry* **CD (track 6). Set your CD player on "repeat" so the track repeats.**

Narrator: The next morning, Pharaoh was UPSET! From the royal palace he called for all of the wise men of Egypt to come at ONCE. He asked the wise men to tell him what the dreams meant. The wise men scratched their heads. They whispered to each other. Finally, the wise men shook their heads sadly. They couldn't figure out WHAT the dreams meant. Finally, Pharaoh's cupbearer spoke up.

Cupbearer: This whole dream thing reminds me of a guy I knew in prison. He told me what MY dream meant. Now what WAS his name?

Narrator: Pharaoh tapped his foot. He cleared his throat. He HATED waiting.

Cupbearer: Let's see, I think his name was Wally. No, that's not it. Fred? It may have been Fred. Nah. Wait! I think it was Bob! Ah, that's not it either. No, NOW I've got it: Joseph. It was JOSEPH!

Narrator: So Pharaoh sent for Joseph. Joseph hurried to the palace and stood before Pharaoh.

Pharaoh: I had some weird dreams last night, and NO one can tell me what they mean. But I hear *you* can tell what dreams mean.

Joseph: No, I can't do that. But GOD can.

Pharaoh: Fine. Whatever. Here goes…

Narrator: Pharaoh told Joseph about the weird cow dream and the weird grain dream.

Pharaoh: I'm thinking it was just a little INDIGESTION. Maybe I should stop eating figs before bed.

Joseph: No, it wasn't the figs. BOTH of your dreams mean the same thing. The next seven years in Egypt will be great—plenty of rain, the crops will grow big, and there'll be LOTS of food. But the seven years after THAT will be bad—no food at all! If I were you, I'd put someone in charge to fix this problem. That person should collect lots of food now so there'll be food during the seven bad years.

Pharaoh: OK—YOU get the job! After me, you'll be the most important guy in all Egypt! Get started!

Narrator: Joseph was put in charge of collecting the food, and there was enough to eat in Egypt even during the seven bad years.

To Talk About

◆ **Pharaoh called on Joseph when Pharaoh needed help. Who has God sent into your life to help you?**

◆ **Joseph knew that his ability to tell what dreams meant came from God. What talents has God given you?**

◆ **God provided a way for Egypt to have enough food during the seven bad years. How has God taken care of you and your family?**

Topical Tie-Ins: Trust, Wisdom, Serving Others, God's Provision

Baby in a Basket

Bible Story
Birth of Moses

Scripture
Exodus 2:1-10

The Scene: a Hebrew home, and the banks of the Nile

The Simple Setup: Turn stage left into the house of Levi by placing several chairs on the stage. Turn stage right into the banks of the Nile by having seated children impersonate reeds and the river. River kids will slowly move their arms like waves, and Reeds kids will hold their arms above their heads (palms of their hands together), swaying.

For Extra Impact: Have River children sit on blue tablecloths, and place the Reeds children along two sides of the tablecloths.

The Characters

Narrator: a friendly storyteller
Levite Woman/Moses' Mom: a girl
Sister: a girl
Princess: a girl

Reeds: children willing to sit and hold their arms over their heads
River: children willing to wave their arms like waves

The Skit

After you've assigned the roles of the Levite Woman, Sister, and Princess, form the rest of your children into two groups: the Reeds and the River.

As the skit begins, the Levite Woman is sitting in a chair, stage left. The Reeds and River kids will be at stage right, in place, doing what they do. The Princess and Sister will be offstage left. Narrator will be offstage, or at one side of the stage, throughout the skit.

Narrator: This is the true account of love, marriage, and how God protected baby Moses. A certain man loved a certain woman, and they got married. The man promised to love, honor, and cherish the woman in sickness and health, for richer or for poorer…well, since they were slaves, there was only POORER…

Levite Woman: Hey—we're poor, but we're HAPPY. THAT'S the important thing!

Narrator: Good point. In time, the woman had a son.

Levite Woman: God has given me such an adorable baby boy. Look at those little, tiny fingers and toes! They are so CUTE! Pharaoh wants us to get rid of our baby boys, but maybe I can HIDE this little guy instead. Let's see…maybe behind the chair?

Narrator: The woman hid her son for an ENTIRE MONTH. But there was a problem.

Levite Woman: My baby is growing! I won't be able to hide him behind the chair any longer. Where else could I hide him? Maybe in the closet?

Narrator: The woman continued to hide her baby, this time in the closet. It worked well for while, but then she saw she had a problem.

Levite Woman: My baby is STILL growing! Plus, he's starting to think he's a COAT! What will I do when he outgrows the closet?

Narrator: The woman continued to hide her baby for THREE MORE MONTHS.

Levite Woman: My baby is strong and healthy, but if Pharaoh's soldiers find him, they'll kill him. I need to find a better hiding place. Let's see…up in the tree? No, that won't work. I know! I'll PRAY and ask GOD what to do.

Narrator: The woman prayed, and God gave her an ANSWER.

Levite Woman: I'll make a strong basket that floats like a boat. Then I'll put little Moses in it and hide him in the river. Nobody will look for him THERE.

Start the "Birth of Moses" track on *The Humongous Book of Bible Skits for Children's Ministry* CD (track 7). Set your CD player on "repeat" so the track repeats.

Narrator: The woman put her baby in the basket and set the basket in the river. The water flowed, and the reeds swayed in the warm wind. The baby's big sister kept watch to see what would happen. The sister hid in the reeds so nobody could see her. She's there now, on her knees so she's almost INVISIBLE!

Sister: If this goes well, I can start my own BABY-SITTING business! Hmm…the baby is fussy. If he isn't careful, someone will find him. Uh- oh! Here comes the PRINCESS! Maybe she won't see the basket! My first day baby-sitting and I'm going to lose the baby!

Narrator: The princess was at the river, and she saw the basket.

Princess: A floating basket! I wonder what could be in it? I'll just push some of these reeds aside and reach into the water to get the basket. Wow—the basket is making noise! Maybe there's treasure inside! Wait…treasure doesn't make noise. Maybe there are PUPPIES! I'll just open this basket and…

Narrator: The princess saw the baby, and her jaw dropped. Her eyes grew wide with surprise. She threw her hands in the air. Then, while her jaw was hanging down, her eyes bugging out, and her hands in the air, she did a little dance of joy.

Princess: It's a BABY! A CRYING baby! Look at those little fingers and toes! He's so CUTE! I want to keep him! I'll name him MOSES!

Narrator: The baby's big sister saw her chance. She walked over to the princess and asked if the princess wanted someone to care for the baby.

Sister: After all, Princess, you don't want to be changing DIAPERS all the time. And babies are messy eaters. And they get into EVERYTHING around the royal palace. I'm sure I can find a kind lady who'd take care of your cute little baby for you. Want me to go look?

Princess: You're right. I could use a NANNY for my new baby. If you know someone, send her around. Right away, too. I think little Moses has a dirty DIAPER!

Narrator: The sister ran home and told her mother that Moses had been discovered. But it was a GOOD thing! Now Moses was safe and his mother could help raise him!

Levite Woman: Not only did God answer my prayer and show me where to hide my baby, but now I'll take CARE of him! I won't have to hide him any longer! THANK YOU, God! Let's go see the princess!

Sister: Mom, do you think people will hire me to baby-sit since I LOST the first baby I was taking care of? You won't mention this to anyone, will you?

To Talk About

◆ Moses' mom must have felt afraid during the months she hid her baby. Tell about a time you were afraid. How did it feel? Who or what helped you to feel better?

◆ God answered Moses' mother's prayer. How has God answered your prayers?

◆ Moses was kept safe because God provided a safe place to hide him. How does God provide for you? How can you thank God for the ways he provides for you?

Topical Tie-Ins: Fear, Prayer, Work

A 911 Call

Bible Story
Moses and the
Burning Bush

Scripture
Exodus 3:1-22

The Scene: a mountain

The Simple Setup: Set up a card table and two chairs for the 911 dispatch operators. Use a large potted plant as the burning bush. Give each operator and Moses a foam cup to use as telephones.

For Extra Impact: Add red construction paper flames to the potted plant.

The Characters

911 Dispatch Operator 1: guy or gal
911 Dispatch Operator 2: guy or gal
Moses: a guy

Sheep: children willing to bleat like sheep whenever Moses or the Dispatch Operators say the word *sheep*

The Skit

After you've assigned the parts of Operator 1, Operator 2, and Moses, ask the rest of the children to be a flock of sheep. Instruct sheep to say "ba-ah" whenever they hear one of the actors say the word sheep.

Place the table and chairs stage left. The operators are sitting at the chairs behind the desk. Moses is stage right surrounded by his sheep. The potted plant is center stage.

Start the "Moses and the Burning Bush" track on *The Humongous Book of Bible Skits for Children's Ministry* CD (track 8). Set your CD player on "repeat" so the track repeats.

Operator 1: *(Picks up phone.)* Hello. You've reached emergency services. What's the problem?

Moses: *(Talking into his phone throughout)* There's been a FIRE. A bush caught fire!

Operator 1: We'll be right there. *(To Operator 2)* Tell the firefighters we've got a bush fire.

Operator 2: Don't you mean BRUSH fire?

Operator 1: No, I mean BUSH fire. We've got a burning bush at…*(To Moses)* WHAT'S the address?

Moses: Mount Horeb, the mountain of God. You won't be able to miss THIS bush. It's on fire, but it won't go out, and it's not burning up the branches.

Operator 1: But that's IMPOSSIBLE, Sir. *(Turns to Operator 2.)* We've got a crack-pot on line 2. Don't call the fire department.

Moses: I was tending my SHEEP *(pause)* when I saw the bush burning. So I left the SHEEP *(pause)* to go see why the fire wasn't burning up the branches. And then I heard GOD talk to me.

Operator 1: I'm sorry, I'm having a hard time hearing you over the sheep. *(Pause.)* It's sounded like you said that GOD talked to you?

Moses: That's right. I'm surrounded by SHEEP *(pause)*, but God DID speak to me. He told me that he was paying attention to the suffering of my people.

Operator 2: Your people are SUFFERING? Maybe we can help. What KIND of suffering are you talking about? Do they need first aid? flu shots?

Moses: They're SLAVES in the land of Egypt. God told me that he CARED about their suffering.

Operator 1: God TALKED to you. You—a shepherd? Sir, you've been in the desert too long taking care of all those sheep. *(Pause.)* I suggest you get into the shade and take a rest.

Moses: I KNOW what I heard. God ALSO told me that he was going to use me to set my people free from their slavery.

Operator 2: Sir, I think you're suffering from extreme dehydration. Sometimes a person SEES things or HEARS things when he's that low on water. We're sending out one of our trained SHEEP *(pause)* to bring you some water.

Moses: You don't BELIEVE me, do you? You think I'm making this all up, don't you?

Operator 2: Sir, what ELSE did God say?

Moses: God said that he'd use me to rescue his people. I'm going to take his people from Egypt to a good land, a land flowing with milk and honey.

Operator 1: Sir, you ARE aware it's against the law for you to call this line and tell us tall tales, right? Voices from the sky…a bush that's burning but doesn't burn up…If you don't hang up NOW, I'm going to have to notify the police.

Moses: But the bush…it's still BURNING. The SHEEP *(pause)* are scared, and the whole MOUNTAIN might go up in flames!

Operator 2: Fine—we'll send out a couple of firefighters to check it out. You'll be there to meet them, right?

Moses: Nope. I've got to get the SHEEP *(pause)* back home so I can get ready to go to Egypt.

Operator 1: *(Sarcastically)* EGYPT? Oh, right. Good luck with that rescuing-a-nation-of-slaves thing. Who knows, maybe that voice will tell you to split the Red Sea or something, too. *(To Operator 2)* Hey—let's go get some lunch. All of this talk about SHEEP *(pause)* has me hungry for some lamb stew.

(Operators 1 and 2 exit stage left.)

To Talk About

◆ **Moses must have been frightened when God spoke to him. How does God communicate with you? How do you feel when God speaks to you?**

◆ **God gave Moses a special job. What kinds of jobs has God given you?**

◆ **If you aren't sure what God wants you to do, how can you find out? Who can help you?**

Topical Tie-Ins: Fear, Listening to God, Standing Up for God, Purpose

All-wet Melodrama

The Scene: a desert
The Simple Setup: You will need no furniture on the stage; an open area where it's easy for the students to move is all you need.
For Extra Impact: Give Moses a staff (wooden broomstick) to raise. Give the Egyptian army cardboard swords.

Bible Story
Crossing the
Red Sea

Scripture
Exodus 14:5-31

The Characters

Narrator: the dramatic reader and director of this melodrama
Captain of the Egyptian Army: a guy or a girl
Moses: a guy

Egyptian Army: kids willing to look stern
Children of Israel: kids willing to celebrate and tremble on cue

The Skit

Melodramas like these work best when there's fun, deliberate overacting. That means exaggerated motions and lines delivered with over-the-top emotion and drama. Encourage your children to have fun with the drama. Be sure your narrator knows to pause after an action is indicated or a line to be repeated is read. That gives the characters time to respond. Consider doing this drama twice so your kids can enjoy it and to allow the lesson to sink in.

As the skit begins, the Captain of the Egyptian Army is at stage left. Moses is at stage right. The Narrator is offstage. Form the rest of the kids into two groups: the Egyptian Army (stage left) and the Children of Israel (stage right).

Narrator: It took 10 plagues before Pharaoh decided to let the children of Israel go, but in time, the Israelites packed up and headed out. No sooner were they out of sight, though, than Pharaoh wanted them back. So he sent out his army—one of the mightiest in the world—to bring those slaves back.

    The captain of the Egyptian Army saluted and said, "Don't worry, Pharaoh. The slaves are as good as gotten!"

Egyptian Army Captain: Don't worry, Pharaoh. Those slaves are as good as gotten!

Narrator: The captain turned to the Egyptian Army. He raised his hands. He said, "Prepare for battle!"

Captain: Prepare for battle!

Narrator: The Egyptian army was brave and strong, but like all armies, they had to warm up before going to battle. All the soldiers did 10 jumping jacks. (*Pause.*) Then they ran in place for 30 seconds. (*Pause.*) Then they all strapped on their armor. (*Pause.*) They pulled on their helmets. (*Pause.*) Then they picked up their swords and spears and picnic lunches. (*Pause.*) Then they stepped into their chariots and buckled up their seat belts. (*Pause.*) Then, with a mighty roar (*pause*)...a MIGHTY roar (*pause*)...they headed off into the desert to go get the slaves. They shouted, "Off we go!"

Egyptian Army: Off we go!

Narrator: And off they WENT, thundering into the desert. Meanwhile, at the Israelite camp, the Children of Israel didn't KNOW Pharaoh's army was coming. The Children of Israel were celebrating by the Red Sea. (*Pause.*) They were celebrating more than THAT. (*Pause.*) THAT'S better! As they celebrated, the Children of Israel noticed that thundering toward them were hundreds of war chariots and troops. The Children of Israel quit celebrating and started SHAKING! They TREMBLED! They opened their mouths and SCREAMED in fear! Moses raised his hands to get their attention.

Moses: Don't worry! Stand firm and you'll see the deliverance the LORD will bring you today! The LORD will fight for you!

Narrator: (*Overly dramatic*) The Egyptian Army is swooping in! The Children of Israel are huddled on the beach, trapped! What will happen NOW? Is it ALL OVER?

Moses: (*Raising his staff—or just his arms*) See what the LORD will do!

Start the "Crossing the Red Sea" track on *The Humongous Book of Bible Skits for Children's Ministry* CD (track 9).

Narrator: God drove the sea back with a strong east wind and turned it into dry land. The waves PARTED, and the Children of Israel walked on dry land. Soon they were safely on the other side of the sea.

Egyptian Army Captain: What's THIS? Hey, THAT'S not fair! We've got you trapped fair and square! Well, if you Children of Israel can do it, so can WE! We'll just FOLLOW you on that dry land!

Narrator: The Egyptian Army got in line to follow the Children of Israel. And at first it went pretty well. Then, when the entire Egyptian Army was in the MIDDLE of the sea, the walls of water on both sides crashed down on the army. See how the soldiers are afraid? See how the army is drowning?

Narrator: When the Children of Israel saw what happened, they couldn't believe it. They all rejoiced! *(Pause.)* They each did a victory dance! *(Pause.)* They jumped up and down. *(Pause.)* And they gave each other high fives! *(Pause.)*

Moses: Trust in God and he will never let you down!

 ## To Talk About

◆ **Describe a time when you felt like God helped you or a family member.**

◆ **How does it make you feel to know that the same God who took care of the Israelites takes care of you?**

Topical Tie-Ins: Miracles, Faith, God's Power

Top-Ten List

Bible Story
The 10 Commandments
Given and Received

Scripture
Exodus 19:1–20:21

The Scene: Mount Sinai

The Simple Setup: You need no furniture on the stage. An open area works best.

For Extra Impact: "Build" a mountain for visual effect by draping a blanket over a coat rack or drying rack. Or provide a sturdy step ladder for Moses to climb (provide a spotter!).

The Characters

Narrator: a friendly storyteller
Moses: a guy

Aaron: a guy
Israelites: guys and girls

The Skit

After you've assigned the roles of Moses and Aaron, explain that the rest of the kids will be the Israelites waiting at the foot of the mountain.

As the skit begins, all of the characters are gathered on one side of the stage. Narrator may be offstage or at one side of the stage throughout the skit.

Narrator: It had been two months since the ISRAELITES left Egypt. They'd set up camp at the base of Mount Sinai. They worked together to set up tents *(pause)*, feed the animals *(pause)*, and cook food over fires *(pause)*. Then Moses, the leader of the Israelites, climbed up the mountain to appear before God.

Moses: *(Pretending to climb)* Hmm…this mountain is a little TALLER than it looked from down below. Good thing I'm wearing my new sandals! I wonder what God wants to SAY to me up there.

Narrator: God called to Moses from the mountain. God told Moses to tell the Israelites that if they'd OBEY God, they could be God's special people. So Moses climbed back down the mountain to report what God said.

Moses: *(Pretending to slip and slide down the mountain)* Whoa, this mountain is SLIPPERIER than I remembered! Good thing my new sandals have no-skid treads!

Narrator: When Moses reached the bottom of the mountain, he motioned for the Israelites to come over to where he stood.

Moses: OK, listen UP, you guys! Here's what God had to say.

Narrator: Moses told the Israelites what God had said. When Moses reminded the Israelites what God had done to EGYPT, they all nodded their heads. When Moses told them that if they obeyed God fully and kept his covenant that they would be God's PEOPLE, they gave each other high fives. Then Moses climbed the mountain again to report back to God.

Moses: Whew, this mountain is DEFINITELY higher than I thought. Good thing my new no-slip sandals are so nice and comfy.

Narrator: After Moses told God what the people said, God sent Moses back DOWN the mountain to prepare the people to hear from God again. So back down the mountain went Moses.

Moses: Here we go AGAIN. Up and down. Down and up. Good thing my new sandals come with a 40-year warranty!

Narrator: Moses waved to the Israelites. He told them to get everything nice and clean, because God would speak again in three days. So the ISRAELITES washed their clothes and got ready for the big day.

Start the "Ten Commandments Given and Received" track on *The Humongous Book of Bible Skits for Children's Ministry* CD (track 10). Set your CD player on "repeat" so the track repeats.

Narrator: On the morning of the third day, thunder ROARED and lightning FLASHED and a cloud came down on the mountain. There was a loud blast from a ram's horn, and the Israelites were SCARED! Their knees shook and their hands trembled, and they covered their heads with their arms. Then God called Moses up the mountain again. Moses trudged up the mountain again.

Moses: I gotta get to the gym more often. These new sandals just aren't doing the trick by themselves.

Narrator: God told MOSES to go back down and bring Aaron up WITH him. Moses stumbled down the mountain. At the bottom, he bent over with his hands on his knees, gasping for air. The Israelites pointed, and whispered among themselves.

Moses: What are YOU guys looking at? Haven't you ever seen an out-of-shape guy trying to catch his breath before? Aaron, c'mon, you have to go up the mountain WITH me. But give me a second here, OK?

Aaron: OK, but…but I don't have any new sandals.

Moses: Trust me, new sandals aren't going to make any difference. Let's go.

Narrator: So Moses and Aaron climbed UP the mountain. Then God gave the people these rules, which we now call the Ten Commandments. You Israelites count along as you hear the commandments. ONE! Don't have any god before me. TWO! Don't worship idols. THREE! Don't misuse my name. FOUR! Remember the Sabbath and keep it holy. FIVE! Honor your father and mother. SIX! Don't kill anyone. SEVEN! Be true to your wife or husband. EIGHT! Don't steal. NINE! Don't tell lies about your neighbor. TEN! Don't wish you had everything your neighbor has. The ISRAELITES trembled with fear, but MOSES spread out his arms and told them NOT to be afraid. And that's how we got the Ten Commandments!

 ## To Talk About

◆ **Moses might not have understood everything God asked him to do, but he obeyed God anyway. When is it hard for you to obey God?**

◆ **God gave us good rules to live by in the Ten Commandments. How would your life be different if we didn't have any rules to live by?**

◆ **God wants us to obey him so we can be his special people. How do you feel knowing that the Creator of the universe cares that much about you?**

Topical Tie-Ins: Obedience, God's Sovereignty

Seeing Is Believing

The Scene: the desert at the base of a mountain
The Simple Setup: You'll need an open area—no furniture required.
For Extra Impact: Teach the Children of Israel a quick circle dance they can do when they're partying.

Bible Story
The Golden Calf

Scripture
Exodus 32:1-35

The Characters

Narrator: a friendly storyteller
Israelite 1: a guy or a girl
Israelite 2: a guy or a girl
Moses: a guy

Aaron: a guy
Children of Israel: kids who'll act along with instructions

The Skit

After you've assigned the parts of Moses, Aaron, Israelite 1, and Israelite 2, ask the rest of the children to be Children of Israel.

The Narrator will be offstage or at one side of the stage throughout the skit. Moses will begin offstage, too. The Children of Israel and Aaron will be at stage left. The two Israelites will be stage right.

Narrator: God's people had been slaves in Egypt before God used Moses to help free the people. God then helped his people cross the Red Sea. God fed his people out in the desert. But still God's people didn't REALLY trust that God would keep taking care of them.

Israelite 1: So how long do you think Moses will stay on that mountain? He's been up there FOREVER.

Children of Israel: Yeah! And is he coming BACK?

Israelite 2: What IS it with Moses? He strolls into Egypt like he's God's gift to the Israelites. Then he ticks off Pharaoh, plagues start landing all around us left and right, and we're kicked out of Egypt.

Israelite 1: That last part seemed like a pretty good deal at first. But then Moses leads us out here in the middle of NOWHERE. He climbs up the mountain and leaves us here. What's up with THAT?

Israelite 2: Maybe we should send up a search party.

Israelite 1: No WAY! If Moses didn't come back I'M not going up there!

Israelite 2: I just wish I could SEE him so I would know he's safe. And I wish I could see GOD, too, so I would know God is still watching over us.

Israelite 1: THAT'S what we need: a God we can SEE. Then I'll feel better!

Israelite 2: We could tell Moses about it, but he's up there on the mountain.

Israelite 1: Hey—you know who we should tell?

Children of Israel: We should tell Aaron!

Narrator: Aaron was the second in command. With Moses up on the mountain, Aaron was watching over the camp. So the Children of Israel went to see Aaron. They surrounded him. They made unhappy faces at Aaron. They shook their fists at him. They stamped their feet. They were UNHAPPY!

Children of Israel: We're UNHAPPY!

Aaron: I can see that. Any special reason?

Children of Israel: We want a God we can SEE!

Narrator: The people pestered Aaron over and over. They jumped up and down and pointed at Aaron. They made their very grumpiest faces at him. Finally, Aaron had listened long enough.

Aaron: OK! You want a God you can see? FINE! Give me all your gold earrings and leave me ALONE. I'll get back to you!

Narrator: Aaron melted down the gold and built an idol shaped like a calf. He built an altar in front of it and threw a party for the Children of Israel. And the people rejoiced.

Start the "Golden Calf" track on *The Humongous Book of Bible Skits for Children's Ministry* CD (track 11). Set your CD player on "repeat" so the track repeats.

Children of Israel: Woo-hoo! At last we have a God we can SEE!

Israelite 1: But isn't that statue just a bunch of melted-down earrings?

Israelite 2: Not anymore. Now it's something we'll WORSHIP.

Israelite 1: Oh. I guess this means I won't be getting my wife's good earrings back, then?

Narrator: God knew what was happening back at the camp. He WASN'T happy about it. God could see all the Children of Israel bowing to the golden calf. God could see them eating and drinking and partying. Look at those Children of Israel kick up their heels! God told Moses that Moses should step back. God was going to DESTROY the people.

Moses: *(Enters from offstage.)* Please wait, God. You've been so good to these people. Give them another chance.

Narrator: God showed his grace by not destroying the people. Moses went down the hill carrying two pieces of stone. On the stone God had placed the Ten Commandments. When Moses saw the people singing and dancing—see them sing and dance?—Moses became ANGRY. He threw the pieces of stone on the ground and broke them. THAT got the attention of the Israelites!

Israelite 1: Hey—Moses! Welcome back! Did you bring us anything?

Israelite 2: I hope it wasn't those stone tablets, because they're all broken.

Stop playing track 11.

Narrator: Moses spoke angrily. He pointed to the people.

Moses: God isn't pleased with you. You've done a wrong thing and made fools of yourselves!

Narrator: Moses took the gold calf and burned it in a fire. Then he ground it to powder, put the powder in water, and made the Children of Israel drink it. See how they're drinking the water? See how they don't look happy? I guess powdered gold in your water isn't very tasty.

Children of Israel: This is AWFUL! Do we have to finish it?

Moses: Drink up! And let this be a lesson to you!

 ## To Talk About

◆ Moses was the leader of the children of Israel. Who are your church's leaders? Do you follow their leadership?

◆ When God didn't work fast enough for the children of Israel, they took things in their own hands. Have you ever tried to make things happen when you should have waited on God?

Topical Tie-Ins: Leadership, Faith, Worship

Mission Possible

The Scene: the edge of a city

The Simple Setup: You'll need no furniture on the stage; an open area works well.

For Extra Impact: Consider giving your spies scarves to wrap around their heads, partially covering their faces, as they sneak into Canaan.

Bible Story
Spies in Canaan

Scripture
Numbers 13:1–14:45

The Characters

Narrator: a friendly storyteller
Moses: a guy
Joshua: a guy
Caleb: a guy

The Rest of the Spies: 10 guys or girls, depending on the size of your class
Israelites: kids willing to act as the crowd of Israelites

The Skit

After you've assigned the roles of Moses, Joshua, and Caleb, form the rest of your children into two groups: the Spies and the Israelites. If you have a small class, kids can play several roles.

As the skit begins, everyone except for the Narrator is gathered on stage right. Narrator may be offstage or at one side of the stage throughout the skit.

Narrator:　　God had rescued the Israelites from Egypt. Now they were almost at the end of their journey—right at the edge of the land God wanted to give them. And MOSES had a game plan.

Start the "Spies in Canaan" track on *The Humongous Book of Bible Skits for Children's Ministry* **CD (track 12). Set your CD player on "repeat" so the track repeats.**

Moses: *(Speaking to Joshua, Caleb, and the other 10 spies)* OK, listen up! God told me to send 12 men, one from each of the 12 tribes of Israel, to CHECK OUT the land of Canaan. To see what the PEOPLE are like, what the TOWNS are like, and what the SOIL is like. Even to bring back some of the crops. Oh yeah, and something else: You have to SNEAK into Canaan. Your mission, should you choose to accept it, is to enter Canaan UNSEEN and UNHEARD. It's a top-SECRET mission. VERY hush hush. VERY important. You've been specially chosen for this mission. Do you accept?

Narrator: The spies shook their heads up and down.

Moses: Even if this is a dangerous mission and you might be CAPTURED?

Narrator: The spies shook their heads up and down.

Moses: Even if when you're captured you're tied upside down and hung from a TREE and people use you for a piñata?

Narrator: The spies looked confused. They didn't know what a piñata WAS.

Moses: Never mind—good enough! You're IN! Now go get that information!

Stop playing track 12.

Narrator: So the 12 spies sneaked into Canaan. They crouched down, looked all around, and tiptoed EVERYWHERE they went. They took notes, and even brought back some of the fruit they saw. The grapes were so BIG, it took TWO spies to carry one cluster of grapes!

Moses: Welcome back! What was it like? Wait, wait, you can't all talk at once! One at a time! You over there, you start. *(Points to a spy, who reads the following line.)*

One of the Spies: We checked the place out, just like you said. And the soil is GREAT—just LOOK at those grapes! But the PEOPLE, well, that's another story. They're HUGE and really SCARY. We don't stand a chance against them when it comes to a fight!

Caleb: Ah, c'mon. Don't be scared. WE can take those guys! Let's go!

Narrator: Most of the spies were scared, and they convinced the Israelites that the people of Canaan were unbeatable. The Israelites were so riled up they wanted to get rid of Moses!

Israelites: Let's go back to Egypt! Enough of Moses! He doesn't know what he's doing! We'd better listen to those spies! I'M not going over to Canaan—no way!

Joshua: What's wrong with you people? If God wants us to have that land, he'll take care of us. Don't be afraid! The Lord is with us!

Narrator: But the people SHOOK THEIR FISTS and STOMPED THEIR FEET. They GRUMBLED LOUDLY against Joshua and Caleb. They were scared and didn't trust God, and that made God MAD. God told Moses he was going to destroy the Israelites.

Moses: Wait a minute! PLEASE! What will the OTHER nations think? Please spare the Israelites!

Narrator: So God pardoned the Israelites—with ONE condition. Not ONE of the people who refused to go into Canaan would ever enter that land. But Joshua and Caleb would! THEY trusted God, and they were eventually allowed to enter Canaan. As for the rest of the people—NO WAY! Their children were allowed to enter Canaan 40 years later with Joshua and Caleb. But during those long 40 years, the Israelites had to wander around in the desert. Just goes to show: It's ALWAYS good to trust God!

 To Talk About

◆ The Israelites were afraid of the people in Canaan. What people scare you?

◆ The Israelites relied on themselves, rather than trusting God. When is it hard for you to trust God?

◆ Joshua and Caleb trusted God and stood up to the other Israelites. How do you stand up for God?

Topical Tie-Ins: Trusting God, God's Plans, Standing Up for God

Barley Bread Battle

Bible Story
Gideon and the Midianites

Scripture
Judges 7:1-25

The Scene: two army encampments

The Simple Setup: A sheet is draped over two chairs to make a tent at stage right.

For Extra Impact: Give the Israelite Soldiers noisemakers and balloons to pop when the Narrator signals them to make noise, and serve bread at the end of the lesson (but be cautious about food allergies).

The Characters

Narrator: a bossy storyteller
Gideon: a boy
Purah: a guy

Midianite Soldier 1: a boy or girl
Midianite Soldier 2: a boy or girl
Israelite Soldiers: boys and girls

The Skit

After assigning the roles of Gideon, Purah, Midianite Soldier 1, and Midianite Soldier 2, assign the other children the role of Israelite Soldiers, and ask them follow the directions given by the Narrator.

As the skit begins, Gideon is stage left, kneeling. Purah is just offstage, stage left. The Israelite Soldiers sit on the floor, stage left. The tent is stage right, and the two Midianite soldiers sit in front of it. The Midianite soldiers pretend to talk together and read a scroll. They ignore the other soldiers.

Gideon: *(Looking up)* Are you sure, God? I HAVE to do this? OK...but why ME? *(Stands and calls.)* Purah! Report in, soldier.

Purah: *(Walks over to Gideon when called.)* Yes, sir. I have the information you requested, and it's bad news. The Midianites are just north of us, and at last count, there are 135,000 soldiers. They're thick as LOCUSTS, sir.

Gideon: How are we looking, Purah?

Purah: We can put 32,000 men on the field, sir.

Narrator: *(Enters; crosses to center stage.)* Hey, that's MY line. Those are MY statistics. You can't do a story without a NARRATOR!

Gideon: So far we've done pretty well.

Start the "Gideon and the Midianites" track on *The Humongous Book of Bible Skits for Children's Ministry* CD (track 13). Set your CD player on "repeat" so the track repeats.

Narrator: Well, I can HELP. Watch! Israelite soldiers, line up. (*Pause.*) Now, MARCH in place. (*Pause.*) Now JUMP in place. (*Pause.*) Now stop. (*Pause.*) See? I can be HELPFUL!

Gideon: OK, Narrator, you can stay.

Narrator: Thanks!

Gideon: Purah, tell all the soldiers who are afraid to fight that they can go home. God wants us to fight with fewer men. I'll fight only with the bravest ones.

Narrator: Some of the soldiers left. All you soldiers who are wearing blue, you sit down. You don't have to fight. Purah looked at the soldiers who were left standing, then he reported to Gideon.

Purah: Good news, Gideon. We still have 10,000 troops left!

Gideon: That's STILL too many. Ask all the troops still here to drink from the stream.

Narrator: SOME of the soldiers got down on their hands and knees and put their mouths in the water. OTHER soldiers crouched down and lifted handfuls of water to their mouths. The crouching soldiers could keep their eyes on the hills around them that way. Nobody could take them by surprise.

Gideon: God wants to send home any soldiers who drank water while on their hands and knees. The soldiers who crouched are true warriors, ready for battle at a moment's notice. How many are left NOW, Purah?

Purah: That leaves us 300 soldiers, sir.

Stop playing track 13.

Narrator: You should be afraid. VERY afraid! The Midianites have 135,000 soldiers and you have just 300 soldiers! That means the odds are…wait…carry the 2…450 TO ONE!

Gideon: Gideon and Purah crept over to the Midianite camp so they could hear what the Midianites were saying.

Midianite Soldier 1: I'm telling you, that dream was so real…

Midianite Soldier 2: You dreamt that a loaf of barley bread was going to crush us in our tents, right?

Midianite Soldier 1: Right.

Midianite Soldier 2: I think that means Gideon and his army will win the battle.

Midianite Soldier 1: WHAT? How do you get THAT out of my dream? I have a dream about a giant pastry and you think our army is going to lose the war? I hope nobody PAYS you to interpret dreams!

Midianite Soldier 2: Hey—it's a HUNCH, OK? From now on keep your dreams to YOURSELF!

Midianite Soldier 1: I WILL. Now let's get some sleep.

(Midianites pretend to sleep.)

Narrator: Gideon and Purah sneaked back to their own camp and gathered the 300 Israelite soldiers around them.

Purah: Israelite Soldiers, are you ready to make some noise?

Israelite Soldiers: Yeah!

Purah: God has given us victory already. We'll surround the Midianite army and shout, "FOR THE LORD AND FOR GIDEON." Let's practice.

Israelite Soldiers: FOR THE LORD AND FOR GIDEON!

Purah: One more time, with feeling!

Israelite Soldiers: FOR THE LORD AND FOR GIDEON!

Narrator: Gideon, Purah, and the Israelite Soldiers surrounded the Midianite army. At Gideon's signal, they all broke the empty water pitchers they brought. The noise woke up the Midianite soldiers.

Midianite Soldier 1: What was THAT?

Midianite Soldier 2: Mommy! I'm SCARED!

Narrator: Then the soldiers all blew trumpets!

Midianite Soldier 1: Listen to that! Battle trumpets! They're getting ready to ATTACK!

Midianite Soldier 2: I TOLD you what that dream meant!

Narrator: Then the Israelite soldiers all held up lit TORCHES.

Midianite Soldier 1: I'll bet there are a whole COMPANY of soldiers behind each captain holding up a torch!

Midianite Soldier 2: We're GONERS!

Narrator: Then the Israelite soldiers all shouted together...

Israelite Soldiers: FOR THE LORD AND FOR GIDEON!

Narrator: The Midianite Soldiers were so frightened and confused that they started fighting each OTHER. It was a great victory for Israel!

Gideon: They're running away! We're winning! Praise the Lord!

 To Talk About

◆ Gideon used so few soldiers that victory could only come through God's power. Why does God want us to rely on his power instead of our own?

◆ God had Gideon spy on the Midianites to help Gideon trust in God's plan. How does God help *you* trust him?

◆ Gideon downsized his army several times to obey God's commands, even though it seemed Gideon needed every soldier he could get. What does God ask you to do that might seem "crazy" to people watching you?

Topical Tie-Ins: God's Power, Trust, Obedience

friends forever

Bible Story
Ruth

Scripture
Ruth 1:1–4:22

The Scene: a field

The Simple Setup: You'll need no furniture on the stage; an open area works best.

For Extra Impact: Scatter the stage with plastic greenery for the characters to "glean."

The Characters

Narrator: a friendly storyteller
Ruth: a girl
Naomi: a girl
Boaz: a guy

Orpah: a girl
Chorus: kids willing to make happy or sad faces

The Skit

Assign the roles of Ruth, Naomi, Orpah, and Boaz. Assign the rest of your children to be in the Chorus.

As the skit begins, the stage is empty. The Narrator is offstage or at one side of the stage throughout the skit. Ruth, Naomi, and Orpah are offstage left, and Boaz is offstage right. The Chorus stands upstage, center stage.

Narrator: Long ago, when the judges ruled in Israel, there was a TERRIBLE famine. NO one had enough to eat. It was very sad...

Chorus: *(Making sad faces)* It was sad. Very, very sad.

Narrator: A man named Elimelech and his wife Naomi took their two sons to another land. Here they come now. See how Naomi is carrying a huge sack of their belongings? See how she's BENT OVER with the weight?

Naomi: Hey, you boys—come help your poor mother CARRY this stuff! Where did those boys GET to? Every time there's work...

Narrator: The family settled in Moab. See how Naomi is setting up a tent?

Naomi: Notice it's NAOMI setting up the tent! Where ARE those boys?

Narrator: Then another terrible thing happened: Naomi's husband died.

Chorus: *(Making sad faces)* It was sad. Very, very sad.

Narrator: But life went on. Naomi's two sons got MARRIED, so Naomi had two new daughters-in-law. One was named ORPAH, and the other was named RUTH.

Naomi: I think I like Ruth best, because her NAME is easier to say! I have two new daughters—how lovely!

Chorus: *(Making happy faces)* It was happy. Very, very happy.

Narrator: Then another terrible thing happened.

Naomi: There seems to be a LOT of terrible things happening lately. Can I get a new Narrator?

Narrator: Naomi's two sons died.

Chorus: *(Making sad faces)* It was sad. Very, very sad.

Narrator: NAOMI was upset!

Naomi: First my husband dies, and THEN my two sons. I think I'll go back to Judah where I came from. I hear the famine's OVER.

Ruth: We'll come with you.

Orpah: Yes, we'll go together.

Naomi: That's very kind, but you girls should stay here in your homeland. I'll be fine by myself.

Orpah: Well…see ya! I like that plan! I'm outta here! *(Orpah leaves stage.)*

Ruth: Naomi, I'm not going to leave you. I'll go where you go, and your God will be my God.

Naomi: Are you sure? It's going to be a LONG trip. And I'm not carrying everything MYSELF this time!

Narrator: Ruth and Naomi hugged each other.

Chorus: *(Making happy faces)* It was happy. Very, very happy.

Narrator: Then Ruth and Naomi trudged back to Judah. Uphill…and downhill. With the wind blowing against them…and the wind at their backs. On and on they went. When they got to Judah, they had to figure out a way to get food.

naomi: Ruth, maybe you could go out to the fields and pick up the grain the workers leave behind for poor people.

Ruth: Would that really be fair to the poor people? For us to take their grain?

naomi: Ruth, look around: We ARE the poor people!

 Start the "Ruth" track on *The Humongous Book of Bible Skits for Children's Ministry* CD (track 14). Set your CD player on "repeat" so the track repeats.

narrator: So RUTH went out to the fields to pick up leftover grain. She bent over to pick up grain until her back hurt. See how she's holding her aching back?

Chorus: *(Making sad faces)* It was sad. Very, very sad.

narrator: While she was working, the owner of the field came over to talk to Ruth.

Boaz: I've been watching your hard work. Why don't you come over and eat lunch with us?

Ruth: Me? But I'm a foreigner! NOBODY eats lunch with foreigners!

Boaz: I know. But I ALSO know how nice you've been to your mother-in-law.

narrator: So Ruth ate lunch with Boaz and his workers.

Chorus: *(Making happy faces)* It was happy. Very, very happy.

narrator: They ate and ate…then they ate some more. They ate until they were full. That night, Ruth showed Naomi how much grain she'd gathered.

naomi: Wow! That's a LOT of grain! Where'd you GET all that?

Ruth: I worked in the fields of a man named Boaz.

naomi: Boaz? You're KIDDING! He was related to my husband! Hey, maybe he'll marry you because your husband died.

narrator: And that's exactly what happened!

Chorus: *(Making happy faces)* It was happy. Very, very happy.

Boaz: Ruth, I'd like to marry you and take care of you and Naomi.

Ruth: Well…OK. Sounds GREAT!

Narrator: So Boaz and Ruth got married. Naomi was so happy she cried—see her tears of joy? Later, Ruth and Boaz had a baby boy. See Ruth rocking the baby? The baby was named Obed. Obed was the father of Jesse, and Jesse was the father of the great King David.

Chorus: (*Making happy faces*) It was happy. Very, very happy.

To Talk About

◆ **Ruth could have left Naomi, but she didn't. When was a time you stuck by a friend even though it was hard?**

◆ **Ruth went out to the fields to gather food for herself and Naomi. When was a time a friend did something nice for you?**

◆ **When Ruth decided to stick by Naomi, she didn't know how things would turn out. But God took care of them. When was a time God took care of your family?**

Topical Tie-Ins: Friendship, Loyalty, Trusting God

Choosing a King

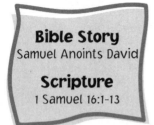

Bible Story
Samuel Anoints David

Scripture
1 Samuel 16:1-13

The Scene: Jesse's home

The Simple Setup: You won't need any furnishings on the stage, just an open floor.

For Extra Impact: Give Samuel a clipboard so he can write notes as he evaluates each brother.

The Characters

Narrator: a friendly storyteller
Samuel: a guy
Jesse: a guy
David: a guy
Sons: seven guys or girls to play David's brothers

People of Israel: a crowd who gives opinions on who should be the next king

The Skit

After you've assigned the roles of Samuel, Jesse, and David, choose up to seven children to play David's brothers. If you have a small class, allow them to double up as the judges. Instruct the judges to read their parts in unison.

As the skit begins, the stage is empty. Narrator may be offstage or standing on one side of the stage through the skit. Samuel will start on stage left, and Jesse, David, the Sons, and the People of Israel will be stage right.

Narrator: This is the account of how Israel got its second king. Saul was the FIRST king of Israel, but because he wouldn't follow God's way, God chose to replace him. God sent his prophet SAMUEL to Jesse's house to find another king.

Samuel: *(Walks to center stage, talking as he walks.)* OK, so I know I'll find the next king of Israel at Jesse's House. But Jesse has LOTS of sons! How am I supposed to know which ONE is supposed to be king? I'd flip a coin, but there's a hole in my cloak and I've lost all my money.

Narrator: When Samuel arrived at Jesse's house, he invited Jesse and his sons to worship God together. Everyone prepared their hearts and worshipped before God. See how they're all bowing their heads in PRAYER? See how they're raising their hands in PRAISE? After worshipping awhile, Samuel told Jesse why he was there.

Samuel: Jesse, GOD has sent me here to choose the next king of Israel. I know one of your sons will be king, but I DON'T know which son.

Jesse: King? One of MY sons? I can't BELIEVE it! Most of my sons can't keep their BEDROOMS picked up, let alone be KING.

Samuel: Well, you can START believing it, because I got the word from God. And there are HOUSECLEANERS at the palace, so keeping socks up off the floor won't be a problem. Now march your sons out here one at a time so I can figure out who'll be KING.

 Start the "Samuel Anoints David" track on *The Humongous Book of Bible Skits for Children's Ministry* **CD (track 15). Set your CD player on "repeat" so the track repeats.**

Narrator: Jesse brought his OLDEST son out so Samuel could examine the boy. Samuel told the boy to flex his muscles. Samuel was impressed by how tall, strong, and good-looking the boy was.

Samuel: This one HAS to be the king. The People of Israel will follow someone like HIM, no question about it!

Narrator: Samuel pictured the people of Israel in his head, encouraging him to choose the oldest son to be king.

People of Israel: THIS is the one. Choose HIM. We can follow someone like HIM!

Narrator: But God told Samuel that the tall, good-looking older brother wasn't the chosen one. God didn't look at people the way others did. People judge each other by OUTWARD appearances, but God looked at what was INSIDE of a person—their thoughts and attitudes.

People of Israel: WHAT? You've got to be KIDDING! This guy looked PERFECT for the job!

Samuel: Jesse, let me see ANOTHER son.

Narrator: So Jesse marched out the SECOND-oldest son for Samuel to examine.

Samuel: Hmm…ANOTHER strong, good-looking young man. He LOOKS like a king. We may have a WINNER!

People of Israel: Choose HIM! Choose HIM!

Narrator: Samuel knew this young man was what the People of Israel were expecting. God spoke AGAIN, and AGAIN told Samuel that this son was not the chosen one. Samuel couldn't BELIEVE what he had to say…

Samuel: Even though this son is tall and strong, and he looks like kingly material, he's NOT God's choice to be king. Sorry.

Jesse: I'd like to remind you that it's the custom of our land for the oldest son to receive the most honor. But you've rejected BOTH my two oldest sons!

Samuel: I know, I know…you got any more sons?

Narrator: Jesse fetched yet ANOTHER son for Samuel to inspect. But again, God told Samuel that this son was not to be the king.

People of Israel: Come ON, already! CHOOSE someone! You're running out of sons!

Samuel: You guys know that you're IMAGINARY voices, right? So what's the HURRY? Pipe down and let me do my work.

Narrator: Jesse paraded his remaining sons in front of Samuel. See how they're standing there looking as kingly as they can look? But each time Samuel's response was the same.

Samuel: Nope. Nada. Nyet! Jesse, don't you have ANOTHER son? NONE of these kids you brought to me are God's choice for king.

Jesse: There IS one left. But he's the YOUNGEST, a shepherd boy tending to the sheep.

People of Israel: A SHEPHERD? NO WAY! There's NO WAY a shepherd could be our king! Let's just call it a day!

Narrator: Jesse found David and brought David before Samuel. Samuel smiled a big smile.

Samuel: This is the one! THIS is the one God has chosen to be king!

People of Israel: You're SURE about this?

Samuel: God looks at the heart—and this is his man.

People of Israel: And we don't get to take a VOTE or anything?

Samuel: THIS is the one!

Narrator: So David bowed down before Samuel, and Samuel poured oil on David's head. The oil was an "anointing," a symbol that God's blessing was on David. And from that day on, GOD'S SPIRIT rested on David.

To Talk About

◆ **The Bible says that David was a good-looking youth also. If all of Jesse's sons were handsome, what do you think was different about David?**

◆ **God told Samuel he looked at what was *inside* someone instead of a person's appearance. In what ways do you judge people?**

◆ **What kind of leader do you like to follow? What do you think God looks for in a leader?**

Topical Tie-Ins: Popularity, Listening to God, Seeing Others the Way God Sees Them

Caution: Watch Out for Flying Stones!

Bible Story
David and Goliath

Scripture
1 Samuel 17:20-50

The Scene: a field

The Simple Setup: An empty stage is all you'll need.

For Extra Impact: Have those in the Israelite Army each hold one color of paper in front of them for their shields and the Philistines another color.

The Characters

Narrator: a friendly storyteller
David: a guy
Goliath: a guy
King Saul: a guy

Israelite Army: children willing to cheer for David
Philistine Army: children willing to cheer for Goliath

The Skit

After you've assigned the roles of David, Goliath, and King Saul, form the rest of your children into two groups: the Israelite Army and the Philistine Army.

As the skit begins, the Israelite Army is at stage right and the Philistine Army is at stage left. David is behind the Israelite Army. The Narrator is offstage or at one side of the stage throughout the skit.

Narrator: Israel was at war, and David's older brothers were in the army. Since they didn't have televisions, radios, or newspapers, David didn't know how his brothers were doing. And there weren't any TELEPHONES, so David couldn't CALL his brothers. David's dad asked David to take some supplies to David's brothers, which meant David was going up to the FRONT LINES. See David coming up behind the Israelite Army? He's getting close to the front lines NOW.

 Start the "David and Goliath" track on *The Humongous Book of Bible Skits for Children's Ministry* CD (track 16). Set your CD player to "repeat" so the track repeats.

David: My brothers should be near here SOMEWHERE. What's that I hear? It sounds like a BATTLE cry!

Narrator: David joined the Israelite Army and saw that across a valley, the Philistine Army was waiting. The Philistines were SHOUTING and waving their spears. And David saw something he'd NEVER seen before. He saw a GIANT—a real-life GIANT! GOLIATH was big, bad, and ready to rumble!

Goliath: Look at you, you scared, little Israelites! Isn't there a man among you who will FIGHT me?

Narrator: David looked to his left. He looked to his right. He expected soldiers, maybe even his very own BROTHERS, to raise their hands and volunteer to go fight Goliath. But not one of the Israelite soldiers raised his hand. In fact, the Israelite soldiers all TREMBLED in fear!

David: Why are you afraid? We can beat Goliath! True, he IS a giant, and he IS carrying a spear the size of my head. And he DOES have a shield so big we could hold a picnic lunch on it. And he IS scarier than anything any of us have ever seen. But we're the army of the living God! That means WE CAN TAKE GOLIATH!

Narrator: One of the King's men HEARD what David was saying, and told King Saul. The King had his men bring David to the royal tent.

King Saul: FINALLY! We've found a soldier who's big enough, strong enough, and brave enough to fight the giant. Now all we have to do is…hey, you're just a BOY. Where's our champion SOLDIER?

David: I'm no giant, and I'm no champion, but I've kept my father's SHEEP safe from bears and lions. God delivered me from those WILD ANIMALS, and I'm sure he'll deliver me from this GIANT, too!

King Saul: Kid, have you actually SEEN the giant?

David: Yes, sir. And with God's help, I'm not afraid.

King Saul: Well, it's YOUR funeral.

Narrator: King Saul decided to let David fight Goliath…

King Saul: Let's get you ready for your big battle. Do you know how to walk on stilts? That would make you TALLER than Goliath.

David: I can't fight on stilts!

King Saul:	No, I suppose not. Well, at least you can wear my armor and helmet and use my sword. THAT should keep you alive for a few minutes.
Narrator:	The King's weapons and armor were too big for David, so he took his staff, five small stones, and his sling. Then David headed across the valley toward the giant.
Goliath:	About TIME the Israelites sent someone to fight me! Hmmmmm. I see a creek…and a rock…and a boy…and a clump of weeds. Where's their SOLDIER?
Narrator:	David walked closer to Goliath.
Goliath:	YOU'RE their soldier? They send a BOY to fight ME? I am going to DESTROY you!
David:	You're a giant with giant weapons, but I have a secret weapon of my OWN! I serve the LIVING God, and today EVERYONE will see that it isn't swords or spears that save us. It's GOD who saves!
Narrator:	Goliath moved CLOSER to David, and David put a stone in his sling. David whirled the sling around and then fired off the stone at Goliath. It hit Goliath in the head! Goliath FELL—facedown in the dirt! The Israelite Army cheered and waved. The Philistine Army turned and RAN!

 To Talk About

◆ Goliath thought that just because he was big, he could beat David. When was a time you saw someone big who was beaten at something?

◆ David trusted God because God had helped him before. How has God helped you in the past?

◆ In what ways has God used you to help others?

Topical Tie-Ins: Fear, Trust, God's Power

Best Buds!

The Scene: a field outside, and an indoor banquet hall

The Simple Setup: Place a tablecloth or blanket on the floor, stage left, for the celebration scene. Props you'll need include a bow (no arrows!), bowls, cups, plates, and plastic fruit.

For Extra Impact: Consider bringing crackers, grapes, or other small snacks for the Celebration Crowd to actually eat.

Bible Story
David and Jonathan

Scripture
1 Samuel 20:1-13, 18-42

The Characters

Narrator: a friendly voice
David: a boy
Jonathan: a boy
Saul: a boy

Arrow-Gatherer: a boy or girl
Celebration Crowd: children pretending to eat and socialize at the celebration

The Skit

After you've assigned the roles of David, Jonathan, Saul, and Arrow-Gatherer, assign the remainder of your children as the Celebration Crowd.

As the skit begins, David and Jonathan sit cross-legged on the floor stage right. The Narrator is offstage. The Celebration Crowd is waiting, stage left.

Jonathan: So you think my dad is MAD at you, David?

David: Look, you're my BEST friend, Jonathan. You know me really well. What have I done to anger King Saul?

Jonathan: I can't believe my dad would want to hurt you, Buddy. OK, my Dad's the KING, so he's under lots of STRAIN. And sometimes he can go a little off the DEEP end. Kings have ISSUES, I KNOW that. But want you DEAD? I just don't think that's true, David.

David: So you think I'm just making this UP?

Jonathan: You've been a good servant of my father. And you're my good friend. What REASON would my father have to hate you?

David: Think about this: Maybe he's afraid I'm going to TAKE OVER. You know how people have always sung songs about your dad? Now they're singing songs about ME, too. Maybe your Dad is…jealous.

Jonathan: I'm STILL not convinced.

David: Look—tomorrow is the start of the NEW MOON CELEBRATION. I always sit next to your dad at those celebrations.

Jonathan: So what?

David: How about if THIS time I hide in the field and don't show up? I'll be SAFER out in the field anyway. Nobody can hurt me THERE.

Jonathan: How does THAT tell us if my dad's out to get you?

David: YOU tell the King I went to Bethlehem for a family reunion. If he says, "That's cool," we'll know everything is OK. But if he goes BALLISTIC and starts chucking SPEARS around, we'll know he was going to KILL me at the celebration.

Jonathan: You're my friend, so I'll do what you ask. But you're going to miss a great PARTY.

Narrator: David and Jonathan came up with a plan. David stayed hidden behind a pile of stones in a field. (*David exits stage left.*) Jonathan went to the celebration and talked to King Saul. Jonathan said he'd signal David by shooting THREE arrows into the field. If the arrows landed off to one side of the stone pile, the King was happy. If the arrows landed PAST the stone pile, David would know King Saul wanted to kill David. David was trusting Jonathan with his LIFE.

(*Celebration crowd enters carrying bowls of food, laughing and talking among themselves. Jonathan and Saul sit together at the edge of the table-cloth or blanket.*)

Start the "David and Jonathan" track on *The Humongous Book of Bible Skits for Children's Ministry* CD (track 17). Set your CD player on "repeat" so the track repeats.

Saul: Fine night for a CELEBRATION, isn't it, Son? I think there are more people here this year than last.

Jonathan: I think you're right, Dad. And the food is GREAT! *(Pops something into his mouth.)* What a FEAST!

Saul: By the way, I haven't seen your friend, DAVID. It isn't like him to miss such a grand meal.

Jonathan: Oh, he had to go to Bethlehem for a family reunion. I told him to go ahead. I was sure you wouldn't mind.

Saul: *(Raises his voice.)* You IDIOT! You're just like all the OTHERS! You'd rather have David as king!

Jonathan: Dad, calm down. Everyone is looking!

Saul: Don't you UNDERSTAND? As long as David is alive, YOU'LL never be king! Go find him and bring him here. I'm going to KILL him!

Jonathan: What has he ever done to you? David is my FRIEND!

Saul: Go get him RIGHT NOW, or I'll kill YOU, too!

(Jonathan runs to center stage. The Arrow-Gatherer joins him. The Celebration People quit eating and watch and listen.)

Narrator: Jonathan knew it was TRUE: His father wanted to KILL his best friend! The next morning, Jonathan told his Arrow-Gatherer to pick up the arrows he was about to shoot.

Jonathan: Start running so you can find the arrows as I shoot them.

Arrow-Gatherer: But if I'm out in the field when you're shooting, won't I get hit?

Jonathan: Don't worry—I'll miss you.

Arrow-Gatherer: Just the same, I'd feel better if I just watch where they go and get them LATER…when nobody is SHOOTING…

Jonathan: Just get OUT there!

Arrow-Gatherer: OK, OK…boy, what a TERRIBLE job…

(Arrow-Gatherer disappears off stage left.)

Narrator: Jonathan pulled back on his bow and shot an arrow into the field.

Jonathan: *(Shouts.)* The arrows are still ahead of you! You have to GO FARTHER!

Narrator: The Arrow-Gatherer didn't know what was going on, but DAVID knew. He stayed hidden until JONATHAN handed his bow to the Arrow-Gatherer and sent him back to the palace. Then David came out of his hiding place.

David: *(Enters from stage left.)* You've been a good friend, Jonathan. You're LOYAL and TRUSTWORTHY.

Jonathan: And you've been a good friend, David. Now we must go our separate ways, but we're both in God's hands forever.

 ## To Talk About

◆ David and Jonathan were best friends. Do you have a best friend? What do you like to do together?

◆ King Saul was very angry. How do you think God feels about people who let their anger get out of hand?

◆ David had to trust his best friend with his life. Who would you trust with your life?

Topical Tie-Ins: Anger, Friendship, Loyalty, Trust

Wise Guy

The Scene: the king's palace
The Simple Setup: a chair at center stage for Solomon
For Extra Impact: Drape the chair with a purple sheet or blanket so it looks regal. Wrap a baby doll in a blanket for Mother 1 to carry.

Bible Story
Solomon's Wisdom

Scripture
1 Kings 3:16-40

The Characters

Narrator: a friendly storyteller
King Solomon: a guy
Mother 1: a girl
Mother 2: a girl
Palace Guard 1: a guy
Palace Guards: kids willing to make announcements and pretend to blow trumpets
Courtroom Observers: kids willing to laugh, point, gasp, and cheer during the trial

The Skit

After you've assigned the roles of Solomon, Palace Guard 1, and both mothers, form the rest of your children into two groups: the Palace Guards and the Courtroom Observers.

As the skit begins, there's a chair at center stage. Palace Guard 1 and Palace Guards are scattered around the chair. The Observers are at stage right.

Start the "Solomon's Wisdom" track on *The Humongous Book of Bible Skits for Children's Ministry* CD (track 18). Set your CD player on "repeat" so the track repeats.

Narrator: There once was a famous King named Solomon. Solomon was famous PARTLY because of his family—King David was his father. But Solomon was ALSO famous because he was very wise. God told Solomon he could ask for ANYTHING he wanted, and Solomon asked for WISDOM. Solomon wanted to be a good king. People came from all OVER to have King Solomon settle their problems. See how there are Courtroom Observers? They're craning their necks and looking to catch a glimpse of King Solomon.

Palace Guards: Hear ye, hear ye. EVERYBODY RISE. Here comes King Solomon!

Narrator: The palace guards opened the great palace doors and blew their trumpets loudly. King Solomon walked slowly, in a very KINGLY fashion, across the palace courtroom. The Courtroom Observers whispered to each other, and pointed at the King. THEY'D heard how smart King Solomon was! Then King Solomon sat in his kingly chair and rubbed his kingly chin, wisely.

King Solomon: Okey-dokey, what's on the agenda TODAY? Do we have WARS to settle? COUNTRIES to make or break? What special problems shall I use my wisdom to solve?

Palace Guard 1: Well, sir, the first case today is about…uh, well, it seems to be centered around…

King Solomon: SPEAK up, my good guard. We don't have all DAY. Out with it!

Palace Guard 1: Well, today's case is about a BABY, sir. It seems to be a case of mistaken identity.

Narrator: The Courtroom Observers giggled behind their hands, and the Palace Guards rolled their eyes and smiled at each other. THIS was new stuff.

King Solomon: Very well. Call the witnesses.

Palace Guards: The court calls Mother 1 and Mother 2. Oh—and the baby, too.

Narrator: Mother 1 and Mother 2 walked up to Solomon's throne. Mother 1 was gently rocking a baby in her arms.

King Solomon: OK, who wants to begin?

Mother 2: I will, your highness. You see, this WOMAN and I live in the same house, just the two of us. I had a baby, and then three days later, SHE had a baby. But one night, her baby died because she rolled OVER on it.

Narrator: The Courtroom Observers gasped and covered their mouths with their hands. The Palace Guards reached for their swords. They thought they might have to ARREST someone.

Mother 2: After her baby died, SHE got up in the night and stole MY baby while I was asleep. She laid her DEAD baby next to me. In the morning, when I tried to feed my baby, he was dead! When I looked more CLOSELY, I saw that it wasn't MY son at all.

Mother 1: It WAS your son. The living baby is MINE, not yours!

Mother 2: No, the living baby is MINE!

Narrator: The two women argued back and forth. They YELLED at each other. They jumped UP AND DOWN. Finally, King Solomon put his hands over his ears.

King Solomon: ENOUGH! Stop! I can't STAND it! Let me see if I have this right: BOTH of you say this baby is yours. BOTH of you say the dead baby belongs to the other mother.

Narrator: Mother 1 and Mother 2 BOTH nodded their heads. The Courtroom Observers looked first at Mother 1 and then at Mother 2. Then they looked at Mother 2 and then Mother 1. The Palace Guards scratched their chins and looked confused.

King Solomon: Well, there's only one way to SETTLE this. Bring me a SWORD!

Narrator: Palace Guard number 1 handed over his sword to the King. The Courtroom Observers held their breaths.

King Solomon: Let's cut the living child in two, and give HALF to one woman and HALF to the other!

Narrator: The Courtroom Observers gasped. A couple of them FAINTED. The Palace Guards shook with fright.

Mother 2: Oh, no, your highness! Give HER the child—please don't KILL him!

Mother 1: It's OK with me—that way he'll be neither yours NOR mine. Divide him between us!

King Solomon: We won't kill the child. Give him to the mother who wanted him to live. She's the REAL mother. Only the REAL mother loves him that much and cares what happens to him.

Narrator: The Courtroom Observers and Palace Guards CHEERED at the King's decision. AND news of the King's wisdom spread far and wide.

To Talk About

◆ When given a chance to ask for anything, Solomon asked God for wisdom. Why do you think he did that? If you could ask for anything, what would it be? Explain.

◆ What special talents has God given you? How can you use those talents for God?

◆ What do you do when you have a problem to solve? Where can you go for help?

Topical Tie-Ins: Wisdom, Problem Solving

Showdown at Mount carmel

The Scene: a desert

The Simple Setup: You'll need no furniture on the stage; an open area where it's easy for your actors to move around is best.

For Extra Impact: Provide cowboy hats and bandannas for the main characters.

Bible Story
Elijah and the
Prophets of Baal

Scripture
1 Kings 18:16-40

The characters

Narrator: a cowboy storyteller
Ahab: a boy to play the bad guy
Elijah: a boy to play the hero

Children of Israel: children willing to bow
False Prophets: children willing to dance

The Skit

After you've assigned the roles of Ahab and Elijah, form the rest of your children into two groups: the Children of Israel, and the False Prophets.

As the skit begins, Elijah is at stage left and everyone else at stage right. Tell children that this is a Western version of what happened; they're to speak with a Western drawl.

Start the "Elijah and the Prophets of Baal" track on *The Humongous Book of Bible Skits for Children's Ministry* **CD (track 19). Set your CD player on "repeat" so the track repeats.**

Narrator: Sometimes you've just gotta show people the TRUTH. That's the situation ol' Elijah found himself in. The people of Israel had turned their backs on God and were worshipping false gods, and God figured to use Elijah to get their ATTENTION. Our story opens with King Ahab callin' out Elijah.

Ahab: Elijah! Is that YOU, you old troublemaker?

Elijah: It shore enough is, you sidewinder. You've been leadin' the people away from God and causing all the trouble YOURSELF.

Ahab: I'm the KING! How dare you talk to me like that?

Elijah: Dare? That's a grade-A idea you got there. I'm callin' you OUT, Ahab! Go round up your prophets of Baal and meet me up on Mount Carmel for a showdown.

Ahab: You think you can take on my 450 prophets all by YOURSELF? You been sittin' in the SUN too long, old man!

Elijah: You're right—those odds are too good. They ain't fair. Tell you what, pardner: Bring along ANOTHER 400 prophets who work for that other false god you worship. What was his name again?

Ahab: You mean Asherah?

Elijah: THAT'S the one—but after our showdown his name is gonna be MUD! God will show you who's in charge around here. Now git!

Narrator: The day of the big showdown came. The Children of Israel—a big crowd of them—had gathered. They all wanted to see the showdown because they knew the odds were 850 to one. Yep—850 false prophets on one side, and Elijah on the other. Those false prophets were ORGANIZED, too. They all had on black hats and wore black boots, because they were the BAD guys. But Elijah wasn't worried. He knew GOD was on his side.

Elijah: You first, sidewinders. Set up your altar, choose a sacrifice, but don't set fire to it. Then you do what you gotta do to get your god to set the fire himself. You do that, you win.

Narrator: So, the 850 prophets built an altar out of rocks. Then they put wood on the stones. Then they cut up a bull, put the bloody pieces of meat on the wood, and started to shout. They shouted...

False Prophets: O Baal, answer us! O Baal, answer us!

Narrator: From morning to about high noon, they shouted and hollered, and there was nothin' doin'. No fire. Elijah started teasing the false prophets.

Elijah: I'm not sure he can hear you! You may want to speak up a bit. Maybe he's taking a siesta and he's asleep. Or maybe he stepped out and headed off to the saloon. Or maybe he's not a god at all!

Narrator: That really got under the false prophets' skin. They danced around the altar, shouting louder. Some of them even cut themselves with swords and spears to show how serious they were. Finally, Elijah had his fill.

Elijah: Enough lollygaggin'. You're wasting' my TIME! This has been quite a show, but it's MY turn now.

Narrator: The false prophets collapsed in a heap. They were sweaty, and thirsty, and tired. But Elijah took 12 stones, one for each of the 12 tribes of Israel, and he stacked them together to make an altar. He piled some wood on top of that, then put his cut-up meat on top of the wood. Then Elijah dug a DITCH around the altar and had some Children of Israel pour water over the whole shootin' match three times. There was so much water that the ditch was full. Then Elijah stepped back and made an announcement.

Elijah: Most of you think I'm plumb crazy soakin' the sacrifice, but I want to make sure you understand something: There's only one God in these here parts, and Baal ain't him!

Narrator: Elijah raised his head toward the sky and prayed.

Elijah: Lord, please answer me so these here people know you are the ONLY law in these here parts. And Lord, show them that you love them, even though they have been slinking around with other gods besides you.

Narrator: At once God sent fire from the sky, and not only was the sacrifice burned up, but also the wet wood, the 12 stones, the soil around the altar, and every last drop of water! God wasn't foolin' around! He wanted to show everybody that he meant BUSINESS! The Children of Israel fell to the ground and worshipped God.

Children of Israel: The Lord—he is God! He is the law in these here parts!

Elijah: Well, I'm glad we got THAT settled. Take them prophets of Baal prisoner, and don't you let any of them get away! Take 'em down to the Valley of Kishon and hang 'em high. We don't want their kind around here NO MORE!

 # To Talk About

◆ **Describe a time you let something get between you and God. What was it? What happened?**

◆ **What would it take to prove to you that God is who he says he is?**

◆ **Have you ever stood your ground as a Christian when the odds seemed stacked against you?**

Topical Tie-Ins: Right and Wrong, Peer Pressure, Standing Up for God

Shall We Gather at the River?

The Scene: two banks of a river

The Simple Setup: You'll need an open area divided diagonally by a "river" of rope or blue crepe paper streamers. You'll also need a paper "scroll" for this skit.

For Extra Impact: Give Naaman a cartoon character bath towel to use after his "bath."

Bible Story
Naaman Healed of Leprosy

Scripture
2 Kings 5:1-16

The Characters

Narrator: a friendly storyteller

Naaman: a boy willing to pretend to be taking a bath

Servant 1: a girl

Israelite King: a guy or girl

Elisha: a guy

Servants: children who will "travel" with Naaman

Waves: children willing to wave their arms as if they're a river flowing

The Skit

After you've assigned the roles of Naaman, Servant 1, Israelite King, and Elisha, form the rest of your children into two groups: the Servants and the Waves. If you have just a few kids, let children play multiple roles.

As the skit begins, Naaman, Servant 1, and Servants are at the river, where the Waves are, stage left. The Israelite King is on the opposite bank on stage right, and Elisha is offstage, stage right.

Narrator: Naaman was a brave army commander who had won big battles. Then Naaman got LEPROSY, a disease, and he began fighting the biggest battle of his life. Leprosy couldn't be cured. Naaman knew he could die, and he didn't know what to do.

Naaman: Why ME? I'm a great guy; EVERYONE says so. I don't deserve this leprosy. I'd do ANYTHING to get well. What am I going to DO?

Servant 1: It's too bad you haven't gone to see the prophet Elisha. HE could cure you.

Naaman: Not funny, SERVANT. NO ONE can cure leprosy. Another joke like THAT and you'll be looking for a new JOB.

Servant 1:   I'm serious. Elisha can ask God to CURE you. God can do ANY-THING.

Naaman: Well, I guess there's nothing to lose…

Narrator: So Naaman asked HIS king to write the King of Israel a letter asking the King of Israel to get Elisha to heal Naaman.

Start the "Naaman Healed of Leprosy" track on _The Humongous Book of Bible Skits for Children's Ministry_ CD (track 20). Set your CD player on "repeat" so the track repeats.

Narrator: Then Naaman and his Servants waded into the river so they could deliver the letter to the King of Israel. The Waves in the river were low at first, but they rose higher as Naaman and his servants walked deeper into the river. The Waves went up to Naaman's knees, then his waist, and finally to his chest. The river was DEEP!

Naaman: I hope Elisha's King doesn't mind that I'm SOAKED.

Narrator: Elisha's King, the King of Israel, read the letter.

Israelite King: Let's see…"To his royal highness." That's ME, so you found the right guy. "I'm sending you my friend, Naaman, so you can heal him of leprosy." WHAT? Is this a JOKE? Nobody can cure leprosy! Wait… NOW I get it! This is a trick. If Elisha doesn't heal Naaman, that other king will declare war on us. If we DO help Naaman, then I've helped that king keep one of his BEST SOLDIERS in shape. He can STILL attack us! What to do…what to do…

Narrator: Elisha heard the King was worried, so Elisha told the King to send Naaman to visit.

Elisha: THEN Naaman and the King will learn that God can do ANYTHING!

Narrator: Naaman and his Servants rode out to Elisha's house, but Elisha wasn't waiting.

Naaman: What's THIS? I come all this way and Elisha doesn't even come to MEET me? No anointing oil? No "take two aspirin and call me in the morning"? Elisha doesn't even bother to SEE me?

Narrator: Elisha's servant told Naaman to go to the river and wash himself seven times. If he did that, Naaman's sores would heal and his leprosy would be gone.

Naaman: Right…like THAT'S going to help!

Servants: If Elisha had asked you to do something HARD, you'd have done it. This is EASY. There's the river, so just do it. Do what Elisha told you to do.

Narrator: Naaman went to the edge of the river and looked in.

Naaman: Seven baths? I HATE baths! Plus, this river is MUDDY! Just look at those WAVES! Back home we've got rivers—CLEAN rivers! Besides, Elisha is ordering me AROUND. He's not the boss of ME!

Servant 1: You want to be healed, don't you? Here, I'll help you get in. (*Helps Naaman crawl in and sit down in the middle of the river.*) Get busy, boss.

Naaman: OK, I guess it can't HURT any-thing. But I'm NOT wash-ing behind my ears! ONE, rub a dub, dub, dub. (*Pretends to scrub arms.*) TWO, splish-splash, I was takin' a bath. (*Pretends to wash hair.*) THREE, don't forget your toenails. (*Looks at arms.*) This is silly; I'm getting out! (*Starts to get out.*)

Servant 1: But you aren't DONE yet. (*Pushes him back.*) C'mon, four. Say "four."

Naaman: All right, but it's NOT working. FOUR, rubber ducky, you're the one. (*Pretends to scrub back.*) FIVE, water, water everywhere. SIX, who lives in a pineapple under the sea? (*Pretends to scrub feet.*) SEVEN, surf's up, dudes, and time's up too. Get me OUT! I'm DONE!

Servant 1: Fine, I'll help you out. You are SUCH a grump! (*Helps Naaman crawl out and stand.*)

Naaman: (*Looks at arms and shouts.*) I CAN'T BELIEVE IT! I'm CURED! I'm gonna go see ELISHA!

Narrator: Naaman and his Servants went to see Elisha.

(*Elisha enters from stage right.*)

Naaman: I'M convinced! Hey—I brought you some money to pay for curing me. Thank you so much!

Elisha: I didn't cure you, Naaman. GOD did. Keep the money, and buy yourself a decent shower cap.

Naaman: It's a miracle! I'm CURED!! Let's CELEBRATE! *(Pause.)* Anyone want to go for a swim?

To Talk About

◆ **What does Naaman's story tell us about God's power?**

◆ **Naaman didn't want to follow Elisha's orders to get well. Tell about a time when *you* didn't want to do what you were told to do to get well again. What did you do?**

◆ **Naaman wanted to pay Elisha to thank him, but Elisha wouldn't accept a reward. Why didn't he take Naaman's money? Why should we help others without expecting to be rewarded?**

Topical Tie-Ins: God's Power, Obedience, Grace

A Simply Sizzling Stand

The Scene: in a city square of Babylon

The Simple Setup: Stack a pile of chairs, blocks or books at center stage for the idol.

For Extra Impact: Drape the "idol" with a gold-colored or fancy cloth.

Bible Story
Shadrach, Meshach, and Abednego

Scripture
Daniel 3:1-27

The Characters

Narrator: the storyteller

Meshach: a guy or girl

Shadrach: a guy or girl

Abednego: a guy or girl

The King: a guy or girl

Crowd: kids who will mime playing instruments and provide verbal sound effects for them

The Skit

After you've assigned the roles of Shadrach, Meshach, Abednego, and the King, designate the rest of your children as the Crowd.

Narrator and the King are stage right. Shadrach, Meshach, and Abednego are standing stage left. The Crowd sits on the floor.

Narrator: It's a cool, pleasant afternoon here in the Babylon city square. You may know that this is the place where announcements are made to the people, and that's what just happened. A government official has just read a decree stating that whenever we hear a horn honking, flute tooting, zither whistling, lyre strumming, and harp plunking, we have to fall down and worship a giant golden statue set up by King Nebuchadnezzar. Anyone who doesn't bow down will be tossed into a fiery furnace. Most people seem fine with the new law, but there are three Jewish slaves who seem to be talking together.

Meshach: Uh-oh. We can't DO that.

Shadrach: What do you mean?

Abednego: I agree—it's out of the QUESTION. This is a NEW robe. I can't just lay down on the ground in it every time some harp player plunks!

Meshach: No, I mean we can't bow to that IDOL. We only worship the one TRUE God.

Shadrach: But what about the FIERY FURNACE?

Abednego: Maybe God won't mind just this once. After all, we don't want to be the only ones NOT doing it. That would be RUDE.

Shadrach: Maybe if we go along now, we can make it up to God LATER.

Abednego: Maybe we just don't have the courage. GOD will understand.

Meshach: Or maybe God expects us to do what is right no matter WHAT. I don't know about you two, but I'M not bowing. Besides, maybe no one will notice us.

Shadrach and Abednego: Yeah, right.

Narrator: Crowd, please stand and get ready to obey the King's command. Listen—we can hear a horn honk. (*Pause.*) And a zither whistle. (*Pause.*) And a lyre strummed. (*Pause.*) And a harp plunked. (*Pause.*) You know what that means—EVERYONE BOW! Look, everyone is bowing, except for those three Jewish slaves. And now the music has faded away and the rest of the crowd is STANDING, and the three Jewish slaves are starting to walk away. That's when someone in the crowd yelled, "Wait! Wait! Not everyone bowed!"

Crowd: WAIT, WAIT! Not everyone bowed!

Abednego: Oh, oh…THIS can't be good.

Narrator: Everyone was pointing at Shadrach, Meshach, and Abednego.

Crowd: THEY didn't bow!

Shadrach: I'm thinking we're going to be hearing back about this from SOMEONE.

Narrator: When the news reached the King, he was FURIOUS.

King: I am FURIOUS! Not just a LITTLE furious, either! I am VEINS-IN-MY-FOREHEAD-BULGING, EYES-POPPING FURIOUS! Bring those lawbreakers here at ONCE!

Narrator: The King had the three Jewish slaves hauled in front of him. The three men stood in a line, Shadrach to the left, Meshach in the middle, and Abednego on the right. No, maybe it was SHADRACH in the middle… no, that's not it. Maybe Meshach was on the left and Abednego was…

King: GET ON WITH IT!

Narrator: Anyway, they were LINED UP.

King: Now, is it TRUE that you refused to bow?

Narrator: The three Jewish slaves nodded their heads "yes."

King: Did you hear the MUSIC playing?

Narrator: The three Jewish slaves nodded their heads "yes."

King: Now, listen CAREFULLY. We'll play the music again. If you DON'T bow, it's fiery FURNACE time for you three!

Narrator: The three slaves stepped back to talk about it.

Abednego: Oh, GREAT. NOW what?

Shadrach: Maybe we should just bow. That fiery furnace looks awfully...HOT!

Meshach: We can't give up NOW. We need to TRUST God for whatever happens.

Abednego: You're right—it's time we took a STAND. You in, Shadrach?

Shadrach: Count me in. I'm trusting God!

Narrator: The three stepped back in line. Meshach spoke for them.

Meshach: If we are thrown into the furnace, our God can save us. But even if he DOESN'T, we will NOT worship your god.

Start the "Shadrach, Meshach, and Abednego" track on *The Humongous Book of Bible Skits for Children's Ministry* **CD (track 21). Set your CD player on "repeat" so the track repeats.**

Narrator: The King was so ANGRY he cranked up the fiery furnace to SEVEN TIMES its usual heat. Then Shadrach, Meshach, and Abednego were THROWN into the furnace!

King: THIS will teach you a lesson!

Narrator: After the three men were in the furnace awhile, the King peered in to see what was happening. He couldn't believe his eyes.

King: Hey, didn't we throw THREE guys in there? How come I see FOUR walking around? And why are they walking around instead of being BURNED up?

Narrator: The King ordered that Shadrach, Meshach, and Abednego be taken out of the fiery furnace. When the door was opened, they walked out, looking just like they looked when they went in. The crowd was AMAZED.

Crowd: Unbelievable!

Narrator: The King walked over to the three slaves and SNIFFED them.

King: This can't be right. You don't even smell like SMOKE and your clothes aren't burned. How is this POSSIBLE?

Narrator: The King scratched his chin. He looked at the furnace, then looked at the three men. Then he looked at the furnace again. Then he began to understand. A big smile lit up his face.

King: Praise be to the God of Meshach, Shadrach, and Abednego, who sent his angel to rescue them. These men trusted their God and were willing to give up their lives rather than serve or worship any OTHER god.

Narrator: The King slapped the three men on the back, and together they PRAISED GOD.

King, Shadrach, Meshach, and Abednego: PRAISE GOD!

Narrator: And the crowd all cheered.

Crowd: Woo-hoo!

 To Talk About

◆ Shadrach, Meshach, and Abednego were strangers in Babylon. Have you ever had to try to fit in to a new place? How did God help you?

◆ Shadrach, Meshach, and Abednego showed courage by their actions. When have you shown courage? What happened?

◆ God spared Shadrach, Meshach, and Abednego. If God hadn't, would that mean God loved them less? Why or why not?

Topical Tie-Ins: Fitting In, Standing Up for God, Courage

Daniel, Daniel, He's Our Man

The Scene: the lions' den

The Simple Setup: Make a simple boundary to represent the lions' den—a line of chairs works well.

For Extra Impact: Have all the "Lions" wear lion masks.

Bible Story
Daniel and the Lions' Den

Scripture
Daniel 6:1-24

The Characters

Narrator: a lion telling the story from his or her perspective

Daniel: a guy

Sam: a jealous supervisor, guy or girl

Lions: kids willing to act like cheerleaders and be funny

Supervisors: kids who will pretend to follow Daniel around

The Skit

After assigning the roles of Daniel and Sam, form the remaining children into two groups: Lions and Supervisors. Assign one of the Lions to play Lion 1.

The Lions are in the den on stage right. The Narrator walks out of the den to center stage. Daniel is stage left. Sam and the Supervisors are stage right.

Start the "Daniel and the Lions' Den" track on *The Humongous Book of Bible Skits for Children's Ministry* CD (track 22). Set your CD player on "repeat" so the track repeats.

Narrator: Hi. My name is Leonard, and I'm a lion. I'm sorry to say that lions sometimes eat people. Not a LOT of people...just SOME people...not all the time...just SOMETIMES. But, starting today, I'm going on a people-free diet! I'll explain why as I tell you the story of Leonard the Lion and Daniel.

Daniel: Excuse me. I think you've got the name of the story wrong.

Narrator: You're right! Thanks for pointing that out, Daniel. It's Leonard the LOVABLE Lion and Some Guy Named Daniel.

Daniel: Not to be rude, but everybody knows the story is called Daniel in the Lions' Den.

Narrator: *(Upset)* See? I get ZERO respect! You make ONE mistake—you eat a few people—and what happens? They name the story after somebody ELSE! What is WRONG with this world?

Daniel: Calm down, calm down…maybe you should just tell the story, OK?

Narrator: Fine. Daniel and the Lovable-Lions' Den. Only, these Lions weren't lovable at all. Not at first. They were fierce and mean with BIG, HUGE, TEETH! See those big, sharp teeth? They were as fast as the wind, rushing around their cage. They held up their claws, pawing at the air. Their claws were as sharp as swords!

Daniel: *(Clears his throat.)* Uh-hmm.

Narrator: OK, claws sharp as those little plastic knives you get at the drive-through window. Anyway, there was this guy named Daniel who loved God. AND there was a king who ruled over an entire country. AND there were some Supervisors who helped the king run things. Wave, Supervisors! God made Daniel REALLY smart and wise. He did a GREAT job helping run the country.

Lions: *(Cheering)* Daniel, Daniel, he's our man! If he can't do it, no one can!

Narrator: Thank you, Lions. That was so good I want to hear it again.

Lions: *(Cheering)* Daniel, Daniel, he's our man! If he can't do it, no one can!

Narrator: Thank you, fellow Lions. Daniel did SUCH a great job, the king wanted to put him in charge of all the other Supervisors.

Sam the Supervisor: Now, WAIT just a minute! He's not the boss of me!

Narrator: Who are you?

Sam the Supervisor: Sam the Supervisor. I supervise the South Side.

Narrator: Sam the South Side Supervisor? There's no Sam in the Bible's account of Daniel's life.

Sam: I know! I didn't even get named, but I'm telling you: I'M MORE IMPORTANT THAN DANIEL!

Narrator: OK, OK! But I STILL think Daniel is our main character, because he served God. That's what this whole story is about. Anyway, the king wanted to make Daniel the boss, and the other Supervisors were jealous. They looked for ways to make Daniel look bad. See how they're pointing at Daniel?

Supervisors: *(Pointing at Daniel)* We're watching you, buddy!

Narrator: The Supervisors FOLLOWED Daniel, but he didn't go anywhere he shouldn't go. They KNELT DOWN in front of Daniel to TRIP him, but Daniel walked around them. One day, the Supervisors saw Daniel kneel and pray, and they said, "AHA!"

Supervisors: Aha!

Sam: That's it! We've got him! Daniel prays three times every day!

Narrator: So? That's not against the law!

Sam: It will be in a minute!

Narrator: The Supervisors went to the king and convinced the king to make a law against praying to anybody EXCEPT the king. If you didn't pray to the king, you'd be thrown into the Lions' den. Why is it always the *lions'* den? What if we're trying to cut down on fat? Why don't they throw somebody into the TIGERS' den for a change?

Daniel: Um, we don't have any tigers.

Narrator: Good point. So, they threw him into the Lions' den. See how Daniel is surrounded by Lions? The Lions ROARED! They were all set to eat Daniel.

Lions: Daniel, Daniel, he's fresh meat! Now we've got a snack to eat!

Lion 1: Before we start, can I have a bib?

Narrator: "Oh no!" the king said. "The Lions are going to eat Daniel! The king was upset, but a law is a law. The Lions OPENED THEIR MOUTHS WIDE to eat Daniel. They opened their mouths even WIDER! AND EVEN WIDER! Oh, Lion Number 2, I think you've got a cavity there!

Daniel: Excuse me! Can we get on with it—I'm about to be eaten here!

Narrator: Just then, God sent an angel to SHUT THE LIONS' MOUTHS. They tried to ROAR, but their mouths were shut.

Lions: *(With mouths closed)* Daniel, Daniel, you're no fun. Without a bite my dinner's done.

Narrator: The king came to the Lions' den the next morning and called out to Daniel. And Daniel called back because he was safe!

Daniel: You've got a lot of hungry Lions in here because God SAVED me!

Sam: Then, the king forgave the Supervisors and gave them all big fat raises, right?

Narrator: Nope. He put them all into the Lions' den where the Lions spent the afternoon MUNCHING and BURPING. And that's the story of Leonard the Lion and Some Guy Named Daniel.

 # To Talk About

◆ **Do you think Daniel was scared in the lions' den? Have you ever had to do something scary? How did you handle it?**

◆ **Why were the Supervisors jealous of Daniel? Why are we sometimes jealous of others? How do you think God wants us to act when we feel jealous?**

◆ **How did God take care of Daniel? How does God take care of us?**

Topical Tie-Ins: Courage, Faith, Jealousy, God's Provision

Man Overboard!

The Scene: a boat
The Simple Setup: Use masking tape to create the outline of a simple boat on the floor.
For Extra Impact: Next to the boat outline, use tape to make the outline of a large fish on the floor next to the boat.

Bible Story
Jonah Flees
From God

Scripture
Jonah 1:1-17

The Characters

Narrator: a friendly storyteller
Jonah: a guy
Sailors: kids willing to be sailors on the boat

Fish: kids willing to "swim" around the outside of the boat

The Skit

After you've assigned the roles of Jonah and the sailors, appoint the rest of the kids to be Fish. If you have a small group, let kids play more than one role.

As the skit begins, the stage is empty except for the boat outline. The Sailors are inside the boat. Narrator may be offstage or at one side of the stage throughout the skit. Fish are outside the boat.

Narrator: Jonah was a prophet of God, and God had a BIG job for him to do. The problem was that Jonah didn't WANT to obey God. God had told Jonah to go to the wicked city of Nineveh to tell the people there to shape up and stop sinning. But Jonah said, "NO WAY!" and ran the other way. Look, here he comes now! Look at how SCARED he looks, and how his knees are shaking, and how he keeps looking over his shoulder like he can HIDE from God.

Jonah: Nineveh! No WAY am I going there—the people there are MEAN! Maybe if I run away, God won't see me. I know! I'll get on a boat that's going in the opposite direction.

Narrator: So Jonah hopped on a boat going to Tarshish. Sailors were hoisting the sails, pulling on ropes, and getting ready to cast off. As soon as they set sail, Jonah went below deck and drifted off to sleep. But up on DECK it was a different story!

 Start the "Jonah Flees From God" track on *The Humongous Book of Bible Skits for Children's Ministry* CD (track 23). Set your CD player on "repeat" so the track repeats.

Narrator: God sent a powerful wind over the sea, causing a HUGE storm. Just listen to the wind blow and the waves crash! The Sailors were so scared they shouted to their gods to SAVE them. THEN the Sailors started throwing all the cargo overboard, piece by piece. But the storm STILL kept up. The wind got even LOUDER, and the waves got HIGHER! The storm was SO bad that even the fish around the boat were getting seasick—look at them turning green! The Sailors didn't know what to do, so they woke up Jonah.

Sailors: Get up! How can you sleep through this STORM? Who ARE you, anyway?

Jonah: Um...well...I...I'm Kermit the Frog!

Sailors: NO you're not! He's green and hangs out with a pig. Who are you REALLY?

Jonah: Well...I...I'm Prince Charming! THAT'S who I am!

Sailors: YOU'RE not charming! Who are you REALLY?

Jonah: OK, fine. I'm a Hebrew who worships the one true God. I've been running away from him—or at least TRYING to.

Narrator: The SAILORS smacked themselves on the head. They knew that if Jonah was running away from the true God, THAT explained the mess they were in. The storm was getting worse by the minute! Jonah and the Sailors could barely STAND because the boat was rocking back and forth so much. The WIND howled and the waves were HUGE! Even the fish in the sea were scared!

Jonah: This storm is all MY fault. The only way to stop it is to throw me into the sea!

Narrator: The Sailors didn't want to throw Jonah into the sea, so they rowed hard. Then they rowed HARDER. Then they rowed harder than THAT. But the wind kept howling, and the waves got bigger. Finally, the Sailors gave up. They picked Jonah up and tossed him into the sea. INSTANTLY, the wind stopped and the waves returned to normal.

Stop playing track 23.

Narrator: The Sailors were AMAZED. They decided to follow God. And Jonah? Well, he was busy sinking to the bottom of the sea, drowning. The fish waved to Jonah as he went past. But God sent a HUGE fish to swallow Jonah up! Jonah suddenly found himself sitting right INSIDE the belly of that fish!

Jonah: Eeeyew! It sure is STINKY in here! And no wonder—look at what this fish has been eating for lunch. There's tuna, and an old boot, sea-weed, and…gulp…I don't even *want* to know what THAT is! I sure have made a mess of things by disobeying God. I guess it's GOOD that I have some time to think.

Narrator: It turned out Jonah had a LOT of time to think about what he'd done. Jonah was stuck inside that fish for three whole DAYS!

 To Talk About

◆ Jonah didn't want to go to Nineveh. When was a time you didn't want to obey God?

◆ Jonah thought he'd be able to hide from God, but he couldn't. How does it make you feel to know that God can see you all the time?

◆ God could have punished Jonah by letting him drown, but God saved Jonah. When was a time God kept you safe?

Topical Tie-Ins: Obedience, God's Provision, God's Omnipotence

A Sheepish Event

Bible Story
Birth of Jesus

Scripture
Luke 2:1-20

The Scene: a field outside Bethlehem

The Simple Setup: The stage is clear except for blocks or books placed on the floor in a circle, to represent a campfire.

For Extra Impact: Cut gray construction paper into "rocks," and place them in a circle on the floor. Tape brown paper into cylinders for "logs," and place them in the center of the rocks.. Angels could wear tinsel halos and shepherds could wear headdress made of towels.

The Characters

Narrator: the storyteller
Angel: guy
Shepherd Telly: guy or girl
Shepherd Smelly: guy or girl
Shepherd Shelly: guy or girl

Sheep: kids willing to crawl around and act like sheep
Angels: kids who would like to be enthusiastic messengers

The Skit

After assigning the roles of the three Shepherds and Angel, assign enthusiastic kids to be Sheep and Angels. The same children could play the roles of Angels and Sheep.

As the skit begins, the stage is clear, except for a campfire at center. The Narrator is off-stage or at stage left. Shepherds are around the campfire, Sheep are on all fours nearby.

Start the "Birth of Jesus" track on *The Humongous Book of Bible Skits for Children's Ministry* CD (track 24). Set your CD player on "repeat" so the track repeats.

Narrator: It was a clear and starry night on a quiet hillside near the town of Bethlehem. Three Shepherds, Shelly, Smelly, and Telly, were watching over their Sheep. The Sheep were restless. They laid down and then got back up. They ate grass. They walked back and forth, so the three frazzled Shepherds couldn't just relax and watch the campfire. One ewe even tried to wander off. See the ewe sneak away from the other sheep?

Sheep: Bahhhh! Bahhhh!

Shepherd Shelly: Hey, EWE, get over here and lay down! BE QUIET! Don't they ever sleep?

Shepherd Smelly: Don't seem to. I should quit this job. Guess I'm just a MUT-TON for punishment.

Shepherd Telly: I know what you mean, Smelly. In the last six weeks I've worn out two pair of sandals, fought off three bears, one hungry lion, and one sheep in wolf's clothing.

Shepherd Smelly: Telly, don't you mean wolf in sheep's clothing?

Shepherd Telly: I have VERY creative sheep.

Shepherd Shelly: Every time I try to count sheep I fall asleep. It takes all my WOOL power just to stay awake.

Shepherd Smelly: I know what you mean Shelly. And how about the way people treat us? You'd think we were criminals. Last week I fell into a pit, and no one would help me out until they realized my dog fell in, too. They felt sorry for the dog, but he wouldn't leave without me. I just want to give up. Why try?

Shepherd Telly: When the MESSIAH comes, things will be different.

Shepherd Shelly: Oh, right. Our people have been waiting for the Messiah to show up for 400 YEARS! Besides, he'll probably just help the rich people. Poor shepherds like us won't even know he's here.

Narrator: While they were feeling sorry for themselves, the Shepherds didn't know that nearby something really AMAZING was happening. Suddenly they saw a great light. An ANGEL appeared, and the GLORY of the Lord shown all around the shepherds. They were SORE afraid. Smelly and Telly stepped back and fell to their knees, but Shelly just stood there.

Shepherd Telly: Hey, Shelly! Aren't you afraid?

Shepherd Shelly: Sort of.

Shepherd Telly: The Narrator didn't say you were "SORT of afraid." You're SORE afraid." That means you're a whole LOT afraid.

Shepherd Shelly: Uh-oh! *(Cowers on the ground.)*

Angel: Do not be afraid, for I bring you GOOD NEWS. Today in the city of David a baby is born, he is CHRIST THE LORD. You'll find him wrapped in cloths, lying in a manger.

Narrator: SUDDENLY, a great number of angels appeared in the sky. The angels PRAISED GOD out loud.

Angels: PRAISE GOD!

Narrator: They smiled and shouted, "GLORY to GOD in the HIGHEST!"

Angels: GLORY to GOD in the HIGHEST!

Narrator: They waved their arms in the air and said "And on earth PEACE to men on whom his FAVOR rests."

Angels: And on earth PEACE to men on whom his FAVOR rests. *(Angels sit.)*

Narrator: When the angels were gone, the shepherds talked among themselves.

Shepherd Shelly: What do you think?

Shepherd Telly: I don't know. What do YOU think?

Shepherd Smelly: I'll tell you what I'M thinking: I'M thinking God answered our prayers! God didn't just tell rich people about the Messiah coming. God told us LITTLE guys, too!

Shepherd Telly: Let's head into Bethlehem and go see that baby!

Narrator: The Shepherds hurried off to see the baby. *(Shepherds walk in place.)*

They found Mary and Joseph and the baby and BOWED down. On their way back, they told people what they'd seen. They shouted so loud that even the SHEEP woke up and paid attention!

Shepherd Shelly: We've seen the MESSIAH!

Shepherd Smelly: We saw the CHRIST CHILD in Bethlehem!

Shepherd Telly: We're not kidding! The LORD has been BORN. Angels told us all about it!

Narrator: When the Shepherds got back to the field, they were glorifying God!

Shepherd Shelly: You're the BEST, God!

Shepherd Telly: We LOVE you, God!

Shepherd Smelly: You're the GREATEST!

Narrator: They praised God for all the things they got to see. They praised God because God did what he said he'd do.

Shepherds: PRAISE GOD!

To Talk About

◆ Being a shepherd was a hard, smelly job, and in Jesus' day, people looked down on shepherds. The shepherds outside Bethlehem must have felt discouraged sometimes. When have you felt discouraged?

◆ God had a plan for the shepherds in the field. God showed them Jesus! What sort of plan do you think God has for you?

◆ The shepherds weren't shy in telling everyone about what they saw. In what ways do you let others know about God's love?

Topical Tie-Ins: Jesus' Birth, Discouragement, God's Plans

Lost and found

Bible Story
Jesus at the Temple

Scripture
Luke 2:41-52

The Scene: Jesus' house, outdoors, and inside the Temple

The Simple Setup: Use stage right for Jesus' house, center stage for the outdoor scene; stage left for the Temple. Place a stool for Mary stage right.

For Extra Impact: Bring several pieces of timber for Jesus to handle.

The Characters

Narrator: a friendly storyteller
Joseph: boy
Mary: girl
Jesus: boy

Head Temple Teacher: a boy or girl
Temple Teachers: a few boys or girls
Traveling Crowd: children to represent the people traveling to Jerusalem.

The Skit

After assigning the roles of Joseph, Mary, Jesus, and the Head Temple Teacher, form the rest of your children into two groups: the Temple Teachers and the Traveling Crowd. If you have just a few children, let the same children play the roles of Temple Teachers and Traveling Crowd.

As the skit begins, Mary sits stage right on a low stool, stage right, stirring something in a bowl. Jesus stands nearby, sanding a piece of wood. The Narrator is offstage, the Traveling Crowd Center is offstage stage right, and the Temple Teachers at stage left.

Narrator: When Jesus was 12, he lived in Nazareth in Galilee with his mother, Mary, and with his earthly father, Joseph. Jesus went to Synagogue school and helped in Joseph's carpentry shop. One day, his mother CALLED to Jesus.

Mary: Jesus, would you come here for a moment?

Jesus: What is it?

Mary: I've been thinking about our trip to Jerusalem.

Jesus: Me, too! I LOVE that we're going to the Passover Feast in Jerusalem!

Mary: Glad to hear it, Son. No question about it—it's going to be fun. But it's ALSO going to be crowded. Your father and I want you to be sure you stay with us so we don't get separated. You're growing up fast, but we WORRY about you.

Jesus: Don't worry, Mom. I'll be sure to stick with family.

Mary: Perfect. That's all I ask. Now go tell your father supper is almost ready.

Jesus: All right.

(Mary and Jesus exit stage right.)

(Traveling Crowd enters from stage right. Joseph, Mary, and Jesus are with them. The crowd slowly moves toward stage left.)

 Start the "Jesus at the Temple" track on *The Humongous Book of Bible Skits for Children's Ministry* CD (track 25). Set your CD player on "repeat" so the track repeats.

Narrator: Joseph, Mary, and Jesus joined their neighbors in making the trip to Jerusalem for the Passover Feast. Thousands of people traveled along the roads to JERUSALEM. People were TALKING. People were LAUGHING. It was VERY crowded.

Mary: Remember, Jesus—STICK WITH FAMILY!

Jesus: No problem, Mom.

(Traveling Crowd stops stage left and starts moving back toward stage right.)

Narrator: When the celebration was over, everyone began the journey home. Mary and Joseph were in the crowd, but Jesus stayed behind in Jerusalem. Because there were so many people, at first Joseph and Mary didn't miss Jesus. They thought Jesus was walking with his friends.

Joseph: Mary, have you seen JESUS? I wanted him to help carry the bedrolls.

Mary: I haven't seen him since before we left Jerusalem. He must be with Joel or Andrew. You know how 12-year-old BOYS can be. They're never in the place you expect them to be.

Joseph: You're probably right. I'll go track him down.

Mary: I'll look too, Joseph. Jesus must be SOMEWHERE in the crowd.

(Mary and Joseph go from person to person in the Traveling Crowd. Each one they talk to shakes his or her head "no.")

Mary: *(Crying)* Jesus isn't here ANYWHERE! What are we going to do? He's been KIDNAPPED!

Joseph: Nobody would kidnap him, Mary. We can trust God to take care of our son. Let's walk back to Jerusalem. We'll ask everyone we meet if they've seen Jesus. And we won't stop until we FIND him!

(As Narrator talks, the Temple Teachers assemble in the Temple. Jesus sits at their feet.)

Narrator: Mary and Joseph walked back to Jerusalem. For THREE DAYS they looked HIGH for Jesus. They looked LOW. They looked to the LEFT, then to the RIGHT. Finally, they went back to the Temple. Jesus was SITTING there! He was talking with the Temple Teachers!

Slowly fade the CD track.

Mary: Jesus! Is that really you?

Jesus: Hi, Mom.

Head Temple Teacher: You the parents?

Joseph: That's us.

Head Temple Teacher: Bright kid you got here. We're amazed at his understanding and the answers he comes up with. You must be very proud.

Joseph: We ARE proud…but that's not going to stop my wife from killing him for wandering off.

Mary: Jesus, what were you THINKING? Your father and I were FRANTIC when we couldn't find you! We thought you'd been KIDNAPPED!

Joseph: Actually, that was just you. I just thought he was LOST.

Mary: Joseph, don't interrupt me! Jesus, we've been searching EVERYWHERE! You said you'd stick with FAMILY, remember?

Jesus: I don't know why you had to SEARCH for me. You should have realized I'd be in my FATHER'S house.

Joseph: Well, he's sort of got you THERE.

Mary: Come with me, BOTH of you. You're BOTH grounded!

Narrator: Mary and Joseph told Jesus to come home with them. Jesus wanted to be obedient, so he went back to Nazareth. MARY, his mother, stored all the memories of what had happened in her heart. Jesus continued to grow, and he was loved by God and the people around him.

To Talk About

◆ **Jesus stayed behind at the Temple. Do you think Jesus was being disobedient to his parents? Why or why not?**

◆ **The teachers at the Temple were amazed at the answers Jesus gave. Why do you think they were amazed? How do you think Jesus knew the answers to the very hard questions when he was only 12? Why do you think he called the Temple his "Father's house"?**

Topical Tie-Ins: Wisdom, Trusting God, Obedience, Searching

A Fish Tale

Bible Story
Jesus Calls the
First Disciples

Scripture
Luke 5:1-11

The Scene: a boat on a lake

The Simple Setup: an empty stage

For Extra Impact: Create a raised area stage right that acts as the boat. Give Simon, James, and John large fishnets.

The Characters

Narrator: a friendly storyteller

Jesus: a guy

Simon: a guy or girl

James and John: two kids willing to join Simon in the "water"

Crowd: kids willing to nod, wave, and shout, "Tell us more!"

The Skit

After you've assigned the roles of Jesus and Simon, choose two volunteers to be James and John and have the rest of your children be the Crowd. If you have just a few kids, let them play both the roles of the Crowd and James and John.

As the skit begins, Simon, James, and John sit on the floor in the middle of the stage. They're pretending to wash their nets. Jesus and the Crowd are waiting to enter from stage left.

Start the "Jesus Calls the First Disciples" track on *The Humongous Book of Bible Skits for Children's Ministry* **CD (track 26). Set your CD player on "repeat" so the track repeats.**

Narrator: One day Jesus was standing by the Lake of Gennesaret with people crowding all around him. The people were listening to the Word of God.

Jesus: Crowd, come FOLLOW me. Let's stand HERE by the Lake of Gennesaret. I want to tell you more about the Word of God.

Crowd: Tell us more! Tell us more!

Narrator: The Crowd LISTENED closely. They NODDED as Jesus talked to them. But the Crowd was so large that many people couldn't see Jesus clearly. See the people in the back standing on their tiptoes? See them jumping up and down hoping to catch a glimpse of Jesus? Jesus noticed the problem.

Jesus: You're a great, attentive Crowd. But I wish more of you could SEE me. Hmm, what can I do?

Narrator: Jesus saw Simon, James, and John sitting by their boats. The fishermen were WASHING their nets. They'd just returned from a night of fishing. A very BAD night of fishing, in fact.

Simon: I don't know why I'm bothering to wash this net. It's not like it got DIRTY or anything. We worked hard all night long and didn't catch a SINGLE fish. Hmph. And now there's a Crowd here scaring away whatever fish might be out in the lake. I am NOT a happy fisherman!

Narrator: Simon looked at the Crowd.

Simon: That's an awfully big bunch of people over there. It's cloudy today, so they can't be sunbathing. And they aren't FISHING. I wonder what they ARE doing. Oh, I see—they're here listening to THAT guy.

Narrator: Jesus saw Simon, and walked over to the fisherman.

Jesus: Simon, can you please take me out a little ways in your boat? That way I can sit in your boat and everyone in the crowd can see me as I teach.

Narrator: Simon did as Jesus asked. Jesus sat in the boat teaching, and the people in the Crowd listened and nodded as they heard what he had to say.

Crowd: Tell us more! Tell us more!

Narrator: Simon was glad he could hear Jesus speak.

Simon: Hmm. This guy has some interesting things to say. Good thing I washed my boat out the other day. I wouldn't have wanted him to see all those fig cookie packages lying around.

Crowd: Tell us more! Tell us more!

Narrator: Jesus finished teaching the crowd…

Crowd: Awwwwww…

Narrator: Then Jesus turned to Simon.

Jesus: Put out into deep water, and let down the nets for a catch.

Simon: You seem to be a pretty smart guy, and I like what you have to say. But, in case you didn't notice, we've been fishing all night and we didn't catch anything. I just don't think the fish are out right now. Might be all those clouds or something. I suppose I could try it though, since you suggested it.

Narrator: Simon THREW out his nets in deep water and when he tried to bring them in they were so HEAVY with fish that they began to break.

Simon: Holy cow! Or, I mean, holy fish! I can't believe all the fish that are in this net. It's starting to SINK my boat! I'm gonna need some help. JAMES AND JOHN, come out here and HELP me HAUL in these fish.

Narrator: So James and John, the sons of Zebedee, came out to help Simon pull in all the fish. When they saw all the fish in his net, they were amazed and FELL at Jesus' knees.

Simon: I can't believe it! This guy is more than a prophet! I can't believe he's standing in my boat. Go away from me, Lord; I am a sinful man!

Jesus: Don't be afraid. Follow me and from now on you will catch men instead of fish.

Narrator: So Simon, James, and John LEFT their boats and FOLLOWED Jesus. They became Jesus' first disciples…and instead of fishermen, they became fishers OF men!

 ## To Talk About

◆ Simon, James, and John were probably feeling pretty discouraged after a night without catching fish. How did Jesus help them? How does Jesus help you?

◆ Simon, James, and John witnessed a miracle and they were amazed and believed in Jesus. What makes you believe in Jesus?

◆ Jesus asked Simon, James, and John to leave everything and follow him. Why do you think they obeyed him? What sacrifices have you had to make to follow Jesus? What sacrifices would you be willing to make to follow Jesus?

Topical Tie-Ins: Jesus the Provider, Miracles, Belief, Cost of Following Jesus

A Feast to Remember

The Scene: a wedding feast
The Simple Setup: You'll need several chairs at center stage.
For Extra Impact: For extra wedding atmosphere, decorate a table with a tablecloth, crepe paper streamers, and flowers. Consider having a cake on the table that kids can enjoy at a "cast party" after the performance.

Bible Story
Water Into Wine

Scripture
John 2:1-11

The Characters

Narrator: a friendly storyteller
Jesus: a guy
Jesus' Mother: a girl
Disciples: a group of guys and girls
Master of Ceremonies: a guy or girl

Servants: a few kids willing to act as waiters and waitresses
Wedding Guests: kids willing to talk together and mill about

The Skit

After you've assigned the roles of Jesus, Jesus' mother, and Master of Ceremonies, form the rest of your children into three groups: the Disciples, the Servants, and the Wedding Guests. If you have a small group, have children play more than one role.

As the skit begins, Jesus and his Disciples sit in chairs at center stage. Wedding Guests, Master of Ceremonies, and Servants are standing near the table. Jesus' Mother is with the Wedding Guests. Narrator may be offstage or at one side of the stage throughout the skit.

Start the "Water Into Wine" track on *The Humongous Book of Bible Skits for Children's Ministry* CD (track 27). Set your CD player on "repeat" so the track repeats.

Narrator: Jesus, Jesus' Mother, and his Disciples had been invited to a wedding celebration in the village of Cana. Everyone was having a good time—a GREAT time. The Wedding Guests were talking and laughing and dancing. Some of them hadn't seen each other in a while, so they hugged each other and slapped each other on the back. The Servants dashed back and forth, putting plates of food on the table and filling everyone's wine glasses. The Disciples were having a good time, too, talking and laughing. Just then, Jesus' Mother noticed something that bothered her.

Jesus' Mother: Jesus, look. The Master of Ceremonies looks upset. Look at how he's waving his arms in the air? And how the Servants are looking all over the room for something? I'm afraid they may have run out of wine. This is terrible! At a wedding feast you're NEVER supposed to run out of food or wine!

Master of Ceremonies: Servants—come here! Huddle up! Has anyone found more wine? No? This is HORRIBLE! I'm going to be SO fired!

Narrator: The Master of Ceremonies took a wine jug and held it upside down to make sure it was really, truly, completely, no-way-to-save-his-skin empty. He SHOOK the wine jug, and not even one drop came out. The Wedding Guests were looking at their empty glasses. Where WERE those Servants who were supposed to keep the glasses filled? Running out of wine at a Bible times wedding was a big deal. It wasn't because people needed more to drink. It was because it was considered an insult for the bride and groom to invite lots of guests and then not have enough wine for them. It would be like you inviting lots and lots of people to your birthday party, opening the presents they brought, and then having your guests share a cupcake instead of a big birthday cake. Running out of wine insulted the guests and embarrassed the people getting married. That's why Jesus' Mother wanted to fix the problem.

Jesus' Mother: Jesus, did you HEAR me? They've RUN OUT OF WINE!

Narrator: Jesus looked at his Mother.

Jesus: Dear woman, that's not our problem. My time has not yet come.

Narrator: By that, Jesus meant the time hadn't yet come for him to show who he was and what he could do. But Jesus' Mother insisted.

Jesus' Mother: Excuse me, Servants? Master of Ceremonies? Please come here. Yes, that's right. Gather around. We need to talk.

Narrator: The Servants and Master of Ceremonies did as Jesus' Mother asked.

Master of Ceremonies: Madam, I'm sure you wish to have more wine, and I want to reassure you that steps are being taken even now to…

Jesus' Mother: Save it, Mister. I know you ran out. I ALSO know how terrible the bride and groom must feel. We can fix this mess, and here's the game plan: Do whatever my son, Jesus, tells you to do.

Narrator: The Servants and Master of Ceremonies turned to Jesus. The Disciples quit talking and listened carefully, too.

Master of Ceremonies: Do you, sir, happen to have a few containers of wine with you?

Jesus: No.

Master of Ceremonies: Perhaps you've got containers of wine outside strapped to a donkey?

Jesus: No wine, no donkey.

Narrator: The Master of Ceremonies turned to Jesus' Mother and looked down his nose at her.

Master of Ceremonies: It seems, ma'am, that your son isn't in a position to…

Jesus' Mother: Were you paying attention earlier? DO WHAT HE SAYS. Trust me on this: It's going to work out. He's quite the boy. I'm proud of him.

Narrator: Jesus stood and pointed to where six empty water jugs stood in a corner.

Jesus: Servants, go fill those jugs with water.

Master of Ceremonies: But we need WINE, not WATER.

Jesus' Mother: DO AS HE SAYS.

Master of Ceremonies: Very well. Servants—hup hup!

Narrator: The Servants rushed to pick up the large jars and go fill them with water.

Jesus' Mother: Boy, that Master of Ceremonies just can't get with the program, can he? You TRY to find good help these days…

Jesus: Good job, Servants. Now dip some out, and take it to the Master of Ceremonies to taste.

Master of Ceremonies: I don't see what THAT will accomplish.

Jesus' Mother: Don't make me come OVER there…

Narrator: The Servants dipped a little into a cup and took it to the Master of Ceremonies.

Master of Ceremonies: Why, THIS isn't water! Where did you get it?

Narrator: The Master of Ceremonies tasted what was in the cup.

Master of Ceremonies: Why, this wine is DELICIOUS! It's MUCH better than the wine we served before! Light, airy, delicate and yet flavorful...I don't know what to say!

Jesus' Mother: How about saying, "Servants, go fill up some glasses before the guests figure out what happened?" What are they PAYING you for, bud?

Narrator: Jesus had turned the water into wine! And not only was it wine, it was really GOOD wine. The Master of Ceremonies was so impressed that he clapped his hands and patted the groom on the back, and praised the groom for saving the best wine until last. The Wedding Guests never knew what happened. They were still talking and laughing and dancing. But Jesus' Mother, the Disciples, and the Servants all knew that something MIRACULOUS had happened. THEY knew Jesus had turned plain water into great wine. This was the first miracle Jesus did in front of people!

 ## To Talk About

◆ Jesus' mother felt bad for the bride and groom, and wanted to help them. When was a time you saw someone in an embarrassing situation and wanted to help?

◆ Jesus' mother had faith that Jesus could do anything. When are times it's hard for you to have faith in Jesus?

◆ Turning water into wine was Jesus' first miracle that people witnessed. Why do you think Jesus did miracles that people could see?

Topical Tie-Ins: Miracles, Faith, Trust in Jesus

Extreme Faith Makeover

The Scene: a yard

The Simple Setup: an empty stage

For Extra Impact: If possible, do this skit near an entrance or in front of a door.

Bible Story
Jesus Heals a
Paralyzed Man

Scripture
Mark 2:1-12

The Characters

Narrator: a friendly storyteller

Friend 1: a guy or girl

Friend 2: a guy or girl

Law Professor: a guy or girl

Crowd: kids who will group together as if trying to enter a house

The Skit

After you've assigned the roles of Friend 1, Friend 2, and the Law Professor, ask the other children to play the role of the Crowd.

As the skit starts, have the Crowd center stage, tightly packed together. The Law Professor will be at the back of the Crowd. Friend 1 and Friend 2 will enter from stage right, holding two ends of a mat or sleeping bag.

Start the "Jesus Heals a Paralyzed Man" track on *The Humongous Book of Bible Skits for Children's Ministry* CD (track 28). Set your CD player on "repeat" so the track repeats.

Narrator: WELCOME to Capernaum. Jesus has come today, and people are PACKING the streets leading to the home where he's teaching. It's standing room ONLY. Actually, even STANDING is hard with so many people rushing to see Jesus. Outside the house where Jesus is, there's a crush of people hoping to SEE Jesus, to TALK with him, and perhaps to be HEALED by him.

Too late to get into the house, some men have arrived carrying a paralyzed friend on a mat.

Friend 1:   EXCUSE us. COMING through. STEP aside, please.

Law Professor: Hey, no cutting in line! We've been waiting here since FIVE THIS MORNING!

Friend 2:   Sorry, but our friend can't walk. We NEED to see Jesus.

Law Professor: So does everyone ELSE in line. What you need to do is WAIT YOUR TURN, just like everyone else.

Narrator: The Friends tried getting around the crowd by moving LEFT, but the Crowd moved left to BLOCK them. Then the Friends tried going RIGHT, but the Crowd moved RIGHT. There was NO WAY the Friends were going to cut into the line.

Friend 2:   What are we going to do?

Friend 1:   Well, we can't QUIT. We've GOT to see Jesus! It's the only hope our buddy has of ever walking again. We should try begging.

Friend 2:   You think that'll WORK?

Friend 1:   What have we got to LOSE?

Friend 2:   Ahem…my dear friends! I know you all have your reasons to see Jesus. I know you've been waiting a long time. But hear me: Our buddy here can't move at ALL—he's PARALYZED! Certainly that MUST earn him a place at the front of the line. Please—I BEG you—let us in! Let us in!

Law Professor: Not by the hair on our chinny-chin-chins.

Friend 1:   Great job. I laughed. I cried. It moved me…but it didn't move THEM.

Narrator: Again the Friends tried to inch closer to the door, but nobody would move. The Crowd just pushed them back every time they tried to elbow their way through the Crowd. The Friends were totally BLOCKED.

Law Professor: WE know our rights! We were here FIRST. Go to the end of the line!

Friend 1:   This is so hard. We're so CLOSE!

Friend 2:   We can't give up, THAT'S for sure!

Friend 1:   I wish we could think of SOME way to get inside.

Law Professor: You and everyone ELSE. What makes YOU so special? Rules are rules, pal!

Friend 1: That guy is REALLY beginning to BUG me.

Friend 2: And you never have bug spray when you really NEED it, do you?

Narrator: The Friends looked at each other and at the crowd. Their arms ached and their paralyzed friend was getting heavy. Would he understand if they didn't see Jesus? If they gave up, what chance did their buddy have to ever get well again?

Friend 2: It's hopeless. We can't go OVER them, can't go UNDER them, can't go AROUND them, and can't go THROUGH them. Let's call it a day.

Friend 1: What did you say?

Law Professor: He said, "Can't go OVER them, can't go…"

Friend 2: I said "Let's call it a day." As in, I give up.

Friend 1: But that's IT! We'll go OVER the crowd!

Friend 2: Great idea!

(Friend 1 and Friend 2 lift the mat over the Crowd and set it behind the Crowd while the Narrator talks.)

Narrator: So the Friends lifted the mat over their heads and found stairs up to the roof of the house where Jesus was teaching. The Crowd didn't try to stop the Friends, because nobody else wanted to get on the roof.

Law Professor: Hey! THERE'S an idea! If you can't get to the front of the RIGHT line, go be first in the WRONG line!

Narrator: The Crowd laughed and pointed at the Friends. But what the crowd couldn't see was that up on the flat roof of the house, the men were cutting a hole in the roof. When the hole was big enough, they lowered their buddy's mat down to where Jesus stood.

Friend 1: Coming down! Everyone watch out!

Narrator: The Crowd pressing around Jesus was surprised—and so was the guy who owned the house! The mat settled to the floor in front of the astonished Crowd.

(Friends arrange the mat or sleeping bag on the floor.)

Narrator: The CROWD couldn't believe the Friends' persistence. What would JESUS say?

Law Professor: *(calling)* Hey, Jesus—tell them to get back in line!

Narrator: But Jesus saw the Friends' faith and said to the paralyzed man, "Son, your sins are forgiven." Jesus healed the paralyzed man's WORST injury first. Not only did the HOUSE get an extreme makeover, but so did the paralyzed man!

Law Professor: Hold EVERYTHING! STOP the presses! Jesus, you can't DO that. You can't forgive sins—only GOD can do that!

Narrator: Jesus told the Crowd that it was just as hard to forgive sins as to heal, but HE could do both. Some people in the crowd weren't convinced, so Jesus looked down at the paralyzed man. He told the man to walk, and THE PARALYZED MAN GOT UP AND WALKED! The Friends started jumping up and down, clapping their hands with joy!

Law Professor: I...I can't BELIEVE it!

Friend 1: Maybe YOU can't...

Friend 2: But WE can!

Friends 1 and 2: THANK you, Jesus!

 ## To Talk About

◆ The paralyzed man's friends never quit trying to help him. Share a time someone didn't give up trying to help you—how did it make you feel? How do you keep trying to do what's right when it gets hard?

◆ Jesus healed the man of his sins first, because of the faith of the friends. Why do you think Jesus did this? How do *you* make Jesus the most important part of your life?

◆ Tell about a time you helped a friend. What did you do?

Topical Tie-Ins: Perseverance, Faith, Friendship

Victory at Sea!

The Scene: a boat on a lake

The Simple Setup: Collect several chairs to create the boat. Fill several spray bottles with water, one bottle for every child who will be playing the part of the storm.

For Extra Impact: Place large box fans on one side of the stage to make wind. Give the Narrator a microphone.

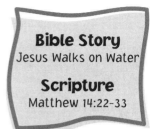

Bible Story
Jesus Walks on Water

Scripture
Matthew 14:22-33

The Characters

Narrator: a squeamish, but friendly, reader

Jesus: a guy

Peter: another guy

Disciples: a group of children who'll say "We're gonna die!" whenever the Narra-tor says the word "storm"

Storm: a group of children who will sway back and forth when they hear the word "storm." They'll also spray water bottles on the same cue.

The Skit

First assign the Jesus and Peter parts. Form the rest of your class into two groups, Disciples and Storm. Instruct children in the "Storm" group to spray their water bottles at the "boat" and to sway back and forth to make "waves."

Make a circle of chairs to create the boat. Have the Narrator sit in the boat with Peter and the other Disciples. Have Jesus offstage at the beginning of the play, ready to enter later. The Storm kids are surrounding the boat.

Start the "Jesus Walks on the Water" track on *The Humongous Book of Bible Skits for Children's Ministry* CD (track 29). Set your CD player on "repeat" so the track repeats.

Narrator: This is your friendly narrator. I'm here in a small, crowded fishing boat with the Disciples. I was hired to narrate the NEXT chapter of Matthew, but I needed a ride to the other shore. Jesus' Disciples are giving me a lift. It's about three in the morning. Most of the Disciples are sound asleep.

Peter: *(Snores loudly.)*

Narrator: Other than Peter, it's very quiet. WAIT! What's this? On no! It's a STORM! The Disciples are waking up. They're rubbing the sleep from their eyes! They're doing what any seasoned fisherman does in a big STORM. They're PANICKING! Oh my. I get SEASICK easily, especially in a STORM with big waves! *(Holds stomach.)* Why couldn't I have narrated this story from the SHORE? I HATE storms!

Peter: What's that out on the waves? Do you SEE it? It's hard to make out with the STORM blowing.

Narrator: The rest of the Disciples looked out across the lake. They saw something that scared them even more than the STORM.

Peter: Is that a ghost?

Narrator: *(Pretending to look off in the distance)* Don't be silly. That's no ghost. It's just a man walking on the water. WHAT?

Peter: It's Jesus!

Narrator: This is too much! A STORM...these WAVES...Jesus walking on WATER, coming toward us. This is AMAZING!

Jesus: Don't be afraid. I'm NOT a ghost! I'm Jesus!

Peter: If you're Jesus, then command me to walk to you...on the WATER.

Jesus: Come.

Peter: Really? This is going to be SO much fun!

Narrator: *(Uneasily)* So Peter stepped out of the boat and stood on the water. The STORM around him raged. But Peter took a few steps toward Jesus.

Peter: Jesus, this is WONDERFUL! I'm walking on WATER!

Jesus: I'm glad you trust me.

Peter: I do, although those waves are REALLY big. And the wind is REALLY strong…Come to think of it, this is impossible. I CAN'T WALK ON WATER! Not even on a CALM day, let alone during a STORM.

Narrator: Peter took his eyes off Jesus and focused more on the danger around him. He looked at the waves. He looked at the STORM. *(Pause.)* And Peter began to sink into the water.

Peter: Save me, Jesus! Save me.

Narrator: Jesus had mercy on Peter. Jesus reached down and pulled Peter out of the water.

Jesus: Why did you doubt my power? Why do you have so little faith?

Narrator: Jesus led Peter to the boat. Jesus and Peter climbed inside the boat. As soon as they sat down, the STORM stopped. The sea was calm again. Thank GOODNESS the sea calmed down. I don't think my stomach could have handled one more wave. All the Disciples began worshipping Jesus and said, "Surely this man is the Son of God." The Disciples quickly rowed the boat to shore, and I for one can't wait! I think I'm going to be sick!

To Talk About

◆ **The storm scared the disciples. What kinds of things scare you? Why?**

◆ **Who do you think you're most like: Peter or the other disciples? Why?**

◆ **Peter trusted Jesus but then lost his trust when he focused on the scary things around him. What distracts you from trusting Jesus?**

◆ **What helps you put your trust in Jesus?**

Topical Tie-Ins: Fear, Faith, Trusting Jesus

What's for Lunch?

Bible Story
Jesus Feeds 5,000

Scripture
Mark 6:30-44;
John 6:1-13

The Scene: a grassy field

The Simple Setup: You'll need no furniture on the stage; an open area will work well.

For Extra Impact: Consider providing blankets or beach towels for your crowd members to sit on. Place several baskets on the stage as well. For extra fun, break apart loaves of bread and serve goldfish crackers during the story.

The Characters

Narrator: a friendly storyteller
Philip: a guy or girl
Jesus: a guy
Little Boy: a guy

Disciples: kids willing to act along with the directions given
Crowd: kids willing to act along with the directions given

The Skit

After you've assigned the roles of Philip, Jesus, and Little Boy, form your children into two groups: Disciples and the Crowd.

As the skit begins, the Crowd is standing stage left. Jesus, Philip, and the Disciples are at stage right. The Narrator may be offstage or at one side of the stage throughout the skit.

Narrator: Jesus had been teaching to big crowds all day. He'd been outside in the SUN, too. At last Jesus waved at Philip and the other Disciples. Jesus was signaling them to COME to him.

Philip: Boy, Jesus must be worn OUT. I know I am! I hope he's calling it a DAY. Let's go see what Jesus wants.

Narrator: Jesus said…

Jesus: It's been a LONG day. Let's get in the boat and go to someplace QUIET so we can rest.

Philip: We're with YOU, Jesus!

Narrator: The OTHER DISCIPLES were nodding their heads in agreement. They were giving each other HIGH FIVES. They climbed into a boat and raised the sails. They rolled up coils of rope. They sat and gently SWAYED as the waves moved the boat away from shore.

Philip: Uh-oh. Are YOU guys seeing what I'M seeing?

Narrator: Philip saw that the Crowd they'd just left was running along the shore. People wanted to keep LISTENING to Jesus. And there were OTHER people coming, too. Maybe the DISCIPLES were tired, and JESUS was tired, but The CROWD wasn't tired! Look at them running in place! Look at them jumping up and down to get a better view!

Start the "Jesus Feeds 5,000" track on *The Humongous Book of Bible Skits for Children's Ministry* CD (track 30). Set your CD player on "repeat" so the track repeats.

Philip: At this rate, they're going to BEAT us to the landing spot. They'll be standing on the other shore when we GET there! Jesus, can't you send them AWAY? They're getting kind of ANNOYING.

Jesus: No, Philip, I have COMPASSION for these people. I'll teach them a little longer.

Narrator: After Jesus and the Disciples reached the shore, the Crowd sat down to get comfortable, and so did the Disciples, but Jesus kept standing. He had to stand so people could see him.

Philip: Master, YOU'RE tired. WE'RE tired! This CROWD is tired. Plus, we're out here in the middle of NOWHERE. Let's let these people go so they can find something to EAT.

Jesus: Philip, where can we get bread to FEED all these people?

Narrator: Philip looked around. There wasn't a store in sight. The other Disciples checked their pockets to see if they happened to have enough candy bars or gum to feed a few thousand people.

Philip: Are you KIDDING? Even if we worked for MONTHS, we wouldn't have enough money to buy bread for all these people! There are THOUSANDS of them here!

Narrator: One of the other Disciples pointed to a Little Boy. The Little Boy had a lunch he'd brought from home. There were five loaves of bread and two fish. That would take care of the BOY, but what about everyone ELSE?

Jesus: Tell everyone to sit down, and ask the Little Boy to come to me.

Philip: You heard the man, kid. Go see Jesus—and take your lunch.

Narrator: The Little Boy did as Jesus asked. He held out the lunch he'd brought and gave it to Jesus. Maybe the Little Boy thought Jesus was hungry, but Jesus wanted the food for ANOTHER reason.

Jesus: You're about to share your lunch, son, but not just with me. You're going to share it with EVERYONE.

Philip: I hate to interrupt, but have you SEEN how many people are in the Crowd? There must be at least FIVE THOUSAND, and that's just counting the MEN!

Jesus: I know. Watch.

Narrator: Jesus thanked God for the bread…AND the fish. Then he told his Disciples to pass out the food to the Crowd.

Jesus: Make sure that everyone gets some.

Philip: Five loaves and two fish? No PROBLEM. We'll be back in about…oh…10 SECONDS.

Jesus: Just do what I say. YOU'LL see.

Narrator: The Disciples walked among the Crowd, handing out fish and bread. And the more they handed out, the more it seemed they HAD.

Philip: This is VERY odd…did I MISS something here? Like maybe a DELIVERY CARAVAN bringing all these fish sandwiches?

Narrator: But it was no trick. It was a MIRACLE.

Philip: Every time I reach into the basket, there's still plenty of BREAD! Same for the FISH!

Jesus: Now go gather the leftovers, so nothing is wasted.

Philip: I'll collect the leftover bread, and you guys collect the fish. I'll meet you right back here.

Narrator: When the Disciples were finished, there were 12 BASKETS of leftovers!

To Talk About

◆ **The crowd followed Jesus so people could learn from him. How can you learn more about what Jesus teaches?**

◆ **When Jesus told the disciples to feed the crowd, they didn't think they could do it. When was a time you doubted that you could do what Jesus told you to do?**

◆ **With Jesus' help, the disciples were able to feed the crowd. What big jobs do you think Jesus wants to help you do?**

Topical Tie-Ins: Miracles, Faith, Listening to Jesus

One Out of 10

Bible Story
10 Healed of Leprosy

Scripture
Luke 17:11-19

The Scene: a village

The Simple Setup: Set some chairs along a road at the edge of the village where people might gather to visit.

For Extra Impact: Draw Bible-time homes on cardboard; hang them on the wall to make a backdrop of a village.

The Characters

Narrator: a friendly storyteller

Jesus: a guy

Matthew: a guy or girl

Leper 1: a guy or girl

Disciples: children willing to act out the instructions given by the Narrator

Village People: children willing to act out instructions given by the Narrator

Lepers: kids willing to follow the Narrator's instructions

The Skit

After you've assigned the roles of Jesus, Matthew, and Leper 1, form the rest of your children into three groups: the Lepers, the Village People, and the Disciples.

As the skit begins, Jesus and the Disciples are center stage. At stage left are the Village People—no, not THOSE Village People! The Lepers are off stage right.

Start the "10 Healed of Leprosy" track on *The Humongous Book of Bible Skits for Children's Ministry* **CD (track 31). Set your CD player on "repeat" so the track repeats.**

Narrator: Jesus and his Disciples were traveling to Jerusalem…

Matthew: Are we there yet?

Jesus: No, not yet. We still have a ways to go.

Matthew: Are we there YET?

Jesus: No. But let's stop and take a break. This village ought to be a good place to find some water and food.

Matthew: And a bathroom?

Jesus: AND a bathroom.

Matthew: Whew! Good thing! I'll be back in a couple of minutes.

(Matthew quickly exits stage left; the other Disciples sit down to relax.)

Narrator: It didn't take long for people in the village to see that Jesus was nearby. Jesus was already famous because of the miracles he'd done—and word spread FAST about him. Look at the Village People—how they're walking over to Jesus. See how they want to shake his HAND? How they want to give him HIGH FIVES? See how they're SMILING? Boy, they're DELIGHTED to see Jesus!

(Lepers enter from stage right.)

Narrator: Wait…now they're BACKING AWAY. The Village People are putting their hands over their mouths like they're afraid of catching a disease.

(Matthew enters from stage left.)

Matthew: Sorry…did anything happen while…AGH! LEPERS! TEN of them! Look at their sores!

Narrator: That's why the Village People were backing away. TEN MEN who had leprosy heard Jesus was outside the village, and they'd come to see Jesus. Leprosy was a terrible disease, and in Jesus' day there was no cure. People with leprosy had to live outside the village, away from their families and friends. It was a VERY sad thing to have leprosy.

Matthew: Jesus, don't let those guys get too CLOSE to you!

Lepers: Jesus, Master, have PITY on us!

Narrator: The Disciples watched as the Lepers called out to Jesus. What would Jesus do? OTHER people had asked Jesus for healing, and Jesus had helped. But 10 lepers? That was asking a LOT.

Matthew: Uh, Jesus, you could always heal them from over HERE. You know, without MAKING CONTACT?

Narrator: The Lepers called out again.

Lepers: Jesus, Master, have pity on us!

Narrator: When Jesus heard the men, he stopped and looked at them. Everyone was waiting to see what Jesus would do. The Village People didn't want the Lepers coming into their village—then OTHER people could get sick. But each of the lepers was someone's husband, son, or father. If Jesus HEALED the lepers, 10 families would be made whole again. Jesus spoke to the Lepers.

Jesus: Go and show yourselves to the priests.

Narrator: That may seem like a STRANGE thing to say, but the law required anyone who had leprosy and then got better to go to the Temple. The PRIESTS checked out healed lepers and OK'd them. Better safe than sorry, you know.

(The lepers exit stage left, walking past the Village People.)

Matthew: Jesus, I know you're in charge and everything, but I've got a SUG-GESTION for you. I'm sure you healed those guys. I mean, you've healed all SORTS of people. But in THIS situation—where there's a big AUDIENCE and everything—maybe you should do something FLASHY.

Jesus: Flashy?

Matthew: You know, some LIGHTNING or FIRE or something. Just sending them to see priests is sort of…BORING. At the VERY least, you could wave your arms and say, "I COMMAND YOU TO BE HEALED."

Jesus: Thanks for the advice, Matthew.

Matthew: No problem. Just trying to HELP. What's a Disciple FOR?

(Leper 1 enters stage left and walks over to Jesus. Leper 1 kneels.)

Matthew: Warning! Warning! Leper on deck!

Leper 1: Master, I'm healed! The priest told all 10 of us that we're healed! I've come to thank you. THANK YOU, Jesus! THANK YOU!

Jesus: Weren't there 10 of you healed? Where are the OTHER nine? Was there only one to praise God? Get up and go; your FAITH has made you well!

Narrator: Faith! Jesus said the man's faith let him be healed of leprosy! The Village People knew they'd seen a miracle. See how they're standing and applauding? The Disciples knew it was time for them to continue on their journey to Jerusalem. See how they're getting up, dusting off their robes, and gathering around Jesus? And now they're starting to walk again.

Matthew: Are we there yet?

To Talk About

◆ The 10 lepers needed Jesus' help. In what ways do you need Jesus' help?

◆ Jesus healed all 10 lepers, but only one thanked Jesus. How have you felt when you helped someone who didn't thank you?

◆ How can you show your thankfulness to Jesus this week? to others who help you?

Topical Tie-Ins: Fear, Thankfulness, Miracles

A Miracle at the Morgue

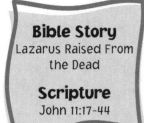

Bible Story
Lazarus Raised From the Dead

Scripture
John 11:17-44

The Scene: outside Lazarus' tomb

The Simple Setup: You'll need no furniture on the stage; an open area where it's easy for your students to gather is best.

For Extra Impact: Break into the church's Easter cantata costumes and props. Without too much effort, you could have a fully costumed cast!

The Characters

Narrator: a friendly storyteller
Martha: a girl
Mary: a girl
Jesus: a guy

Lazarus: a guy
Funeral Director: a guy or girl who can project a snooty attitude
Mourners: children willing to act sad

The Skit

After you've assigned the roles of Martha, Mary, Jesus, Lazarus, and the Funeral Director, ask the remaining children to play the role of Mourners.

Start the "Lazarus Raised From the Dead" track on *The Humongous Book of Bible Skits for Children's Ministry* **CD (track 32). Set your CD player on "repeat" so the track repeats.**

As the skit starts, Mary, Martha, and Lazarus are at stage left. So are the Mourners. Lazarus is lying flat on the floor. Jesus enters from stage right.

Narrator: Jesus had been called to the home of Lazarus, a very close friend. The reason was sad—Lazarus had DIED just days before.

Funeral Director: Good afternoon, sir. I am the Funeral Director. Are you a friend of the family?

Jesus: Yes, I am.

Martha: Jesus, I'm so GLAD you're here. We've been expecting you for DAYS. If you had been here earlier, Lazarus wouldn't have died. Why didn't you COME?

Jesus: Don't worry, Martha. Your brother will rise again.

Martha: I know that, but waiting until the resurrection doesn't help me NOW. I'm so SAD.

Jesus: You don't have to wait. I AM that resurrection.

Martha: Jesus, you ARE the Messiah, the Son of God.

Funeral Director: Then you're a VERY special guest. Should I seat Jesus with the family?

Jesus: Is Mary here?

Martha: Mary! The TEACHER is here, and he's asking for you.

Mary: I can't believe Lazarus is dead. I can't believe he's GONE. Jesus, if you'd just been here…

Martha: I already told him that.

Jesus: Where IS Lazarus?

Funeral Director: If you'd step this way, please. We've prepared the body and sealed the tomb, but I can show you the grave site.

Mourners: We can't believe Lazarus is dead! We can't believe he's gone!

Jesus: Open the tomb.

Funeral Director: Sir. You don't understand…

Jesus: No, it's YOU who doesn't understand. Open the tomb.

Martha: By the way, since there WEREN'T any funeral directors in Bible times, and dead people were buried within 24 hours, what is that Funeral Director DOING here?

Narrator: He's here to help our skit move along faster. He doesn't really EXIST.

Martha: OK. Just wanted to clear that up.

Funeral Director: So much for job security…

Mary: Jesus, my brother has been dead for FOUR days.

Funeral Director: The body is going to be decaying by now, sir. If you open that tomb, there's going to be a BIG stink.

Jesus: If you don't LEAVE, there's going to be a big stink. Open the tomb and leave. You are NOT needed here.

Funeral Director: Very well, sir. We'll move the stone over the tomb. It's YOUR funeral—so to speak.

Narrator: As the tomb of Lazarus was being opened, the Mourners looked at Jesus. Jesus was WEEPING. He truly loved Lazarus. Then Jesus stood and faced the tomb. Jesus called out words nobody thought they'd hear.

Jesus: *(With authority)* LAZARUS. COME OUT!

Lazarus: Are you calling me?

Jesus: Yes, I'm calling you. Get OUT here!

Lazarus: Coming! I'm just a little…tied up. Why am I wearing grave wrappings? What's going ON here?

Funeral Director: Wait—that man was DEAD. I BURIED him!

Jesus: Like I said, you aren't needed here. I am the resurrection and the life, and one of these days I'll put death TOTALLY out of business.

Narrator: The Mourners were ASTOUNDED! They jumped with joy! They raised their hands and praised God!

Funeral Director: Jesus, even though I don't really exist, I hope you don't do away with death any time soon. Then I'll REALLY be out of a job!

Jesus: *(Hugging Lazarus)* I am SO glad to see you, friend.

Lazarus: I'm glad to see you, TOO. Man, what HAPPENED? I slept like the DEAD last night.

Jesus: Not just last night. We're talking DAYS.

Martha: Come on home, brother. We'll tell you more over DINNER.

Funeral Director: *(Calling after Lazarus)* I hope you realize I'm not giving you a REFUND on this funeral!

To Talk About

◆ Have you ever had someone close to you die? Why do you think having a loved one die hurts us so much?

◆ Jesus wept at the tomb of his good friend Lazarus. How does it make you feel to know that Jesus hurts for us when we hurt?

◆ How can we trust Jesus when we hurt?

Topical Tie-Ins: Death, Resurrection, Compassion

Construction Site

Bible Story
Wise and Foolish
Builders

Scripture
Matthew 7:24-29

The Scene: a construction site

The Simple Setup: You'll need no furniture on the stage; an open area works well.

For Extra Impact: Consider giving your Builders plastic hard hats (available at party stores). Give your Rain characters spray bottles of water and your Wind characters sheets of paper to wave.

The Characters

Narrator: a friendly storyteller

Jesus: a guy

Wise Builder: a guy or girl

Foolish Builder: a guy or girl

Solid House: two or more kids willing to join hands in the air to form the peak of a strong house

Weak House: two or more kids willing to join hands in the air to form the peak of a house that collapses

Rain: kids willing to wiggle their fingers as raindrops

Wind: kids willing to make sound effects of blowing wind

The Skit

After you've assigned the roles of Jesus and the two Builders, form the rest of your children into four groups: the Solid House, the Weak House, the Rain, and the Wind. If you have just a few children, let them play multiple roles.

As the skit begins, the stage is empty except for Jesus. Narrator may be offstage or at one side of the stage throughout the skit. The other roles take center stage when directed by the Narrator.

Narrator: One day, Jesus was sharing with people why they should follow his teachings.

Jesus: Anyone who listens to my teaching and follows it is like a WISE Builder who built a house on solid ROCK.

Wise Builder: La de dah…I think I'll build a new house today. But first I need to find a good spot. How about that land over there, close to the beach? It's got a GREAT view of the ocean! You could almost go fishing right out the WINDOW! Hmm. The ground feels kind of squishy—like it's SAND. I don't think THAT would be a very good idea! The first good rain would wash away the sand AND my house. No siree, I'm not building MY house on sand. Ah, THAT spot looks much better. It's solid ROCK!

Narrator: The Wise Builder put the pieces of his house together. See HOW solid the Solid House is? The Wise Builder is leaning against it and it doesn't move at all. Jesus also talked about ANOTHER builder.

Jesus: Anyone who hears my teaching and IGNORES it is foolish, like a FOOLISH Builder who builds a house on sand.

Foolish Builder: Where, oh where, to build my new house? I guess it really doesn't matter. Land IS land, you know? This spot looks good. Nice and soft. I won't have to work so hard.

Narrator: The Foolish Builder looked over at the Wise Builder.

Foolish Builder: What a dummy! He built his house on hard ROCK. That must have taken FOREVER! I'm glad I found the *perfect* spot!

Start the "Wise and Foolish Builders" track on *The Humongous Book of Bible Skits for Children's Ministry* **CD (track 33). Set your CD player on "repeat" so the track repeats.**

Jesus: Then one day the RAIN fell. It rained so hard you could barely see. And the WIND pushed against the houses. When that happened, which house do you think was still STANDING when the storm had passed?

Wise Builder: *(Sitting in his house)* Whoa, this is SOME storm! Just listen to that WIND roar! And so much RAIN! It's pounding on my roof and running all around my house!

Foolish Builder: *(Sitting in his house)* Wow, listen to that RAIN! It's a DOWNPOUR! It's flooding all around my house! And that WIND! I can feel the walls shaking! Yikes, it feels like I'm tilting! What's HAPPENING?

Jesus: The SOLID HOUSE didn't collapse, because it was built on rock. The SOLID HOUSE stood strong. But the WEAK HOUSE fell to pieces and hit the ground with a mighty CRASH!

Narrator: When the people listening to Jesus heard what he had to say, they were amazed. He KNEW what he was talking about! He should—he's the Master Builder!

 To Talk About

◆ What do you think it means to build your life on a solid foundation? What would you use as a strong foundation?

◆ What kinds of weak things do people build their lives on? How can you avoid building your life on a weak foundation?

◆ How can you learn more about what Jesus wants you to do?

Topical Tie-Ins: Wisdom, Obedience

Nothing But Net—Worth

The Scene: a courtyard

The Simple Setup: You'll need a table with a box on it at center stage.

For Extra Impact: Gift wrap the outside of a large, open box as an offering box, and let the Givers place offerings such as stuffed animals, keys, books, and clothing into the this box to symbolize their gifts to God.

Bible Story
Widow's Offering

Scripture
Mark 12:41-44

The Characters

Narrator: a sports announcer

Jesus: a boy

James: a boy or girl

Widow: a girl

Disciples: boys and girls

Givers: boys and girls

The Skit

After you've assigned the roles of Jesus, James, and the Widow, form children into two groups: Disciples and Givers.

As the skit begins, the Disciples and Jesus are at stage left, and the Givers and the Widow are at stage right. The box sits on a table center stage. The Narrator will be at one side of the stage throughout the skit.

Start the "Widow's Offering" track on *The Humongous Book of Bible Skits for Children's Ministry* CD (track 34). Set your CD player on "repeat" so the track repeats.

Narrator: We're here at the Temple, watching an offering box. There's NO defense at all, and it's OPEN SEASON on the box! Anyone wanting to drop in a coin or two or 10 has a CLEAR shot! Jesus is standing to one side with his Disciples. They're watching as one after another, Givers are SCORING points by dropping in coins!

Jesus: Tell me, what do you see?

James: Um…I see people dropping coins into a box. Should I be seeing something ELSE?

Narrator: Folks, here's what I see: a veritable PARADE of Givers! One Giver is approaching the box now and SLAM-DUNKING in a handful of coins! Now ANOTHER Giver is making a move—but she's pulling up short of the box. She's taking a THREE-POINT SHOT and it is…GOOD! WHAT A SHOT! She's doing a little victory dance! Now MORE Givers are SWARMING the box! It's a GREAT day for the church! The money is POURING in!

James: I mean, people are dropping in their offerings, right? Can't have church without an offering, right?

Jesus: Keep watching. You can learn a LOT by watching people give.

Narrator: Now, THIS Giver is going back…back…BACK into his wallet. AWESOME, BA-BY! It hits the rim, but it's STILL a score! And LOOK AT ALL THOSE COINS! Wow—that's a Giver who's going ALL the way! It's TITHE PLUS! WOW! Look at the Disciples—they're APPLAUDING!

James: What an OFFERING! You must be VERY pleased with that one—I've never SEEN so much money!

Jesus: It's not so much to him. Or me.

Narrator: Whoa, TOUGH crowd. This JESUS doesn't impress EASILY. I'd hate to think how much it takes to get HIS attention. Any more GIVERS? Wait, look who's coming up to the box…There's a WIDOW shuffling up to take her shot. She looks left, then right, I think she's going to sneak it in the box. She goes up and HERE'S THE PAYOFF! Oh, man, WHAT a letdown! TWO COPPER COINS! Less than a PENNY! Hardly worth the EFFORT! How could she put in so LITTLE when everyone else has given SO MUCH?

Jesus: That widow is the person I wanted you to see today.

James: Oh, I get it. She's in TROUBLE. You're DISAPPOINTED with her, aren't you?

Jesus: DISAPPOINTED? Not at all!

James: But her gift doesn't BEGIN to compare to the other gifts, Jesus.

Jesus: Precisely. HERS was BEST.

Narrator: You've got to be KIDDING! Time for a T-O. TIME OUT! I don't understand this at ALL. Ma'am, will you shuffle on over here? A quick question: Exactly how much did you put in the offering box?

Widow: Just a few copper coins.

Narrator: I THOUGHT so.

Widow: When I saw how much OTHER people were putting in, I was a little ashamed. I wish it was more, I really do. But I gave everything I had. EVERYTHING.

James: Jesus, what about the OTHER Givers? They gave more; I SAW it.

Jesus: I tell you the truth, this poor widow has put MORE in the treasury than all the others. They gave out of their wealth. She gave out of her poverty. She put in everything she has to live on.

James: Oh…guess I didn't think about that.

Narrator: Me either. Sorry, ma'am.

Widow: That's all right. But here's some good advice for you, Narrator.

Narrator: What's that?

Widow: Quit watching what people put in the offering box! It's RUDE!

Narrator: Yes, ma'am.

Widow: And quit bothering old ladies!

Narrator: Yes, ma'am.

Widow: And do something about that hair! Get a haircut!

Narrator: Yes, ma'am. Anything else?

Widow: (*Sweetly*) No, dear. That should cover it.

Narrator: So there you have it—ringside here at the offering box in the Temple, and it's…

Widow: And don't talk so fast!

To Talk About

◆ Jesus watched what everyone gave at the Temple. How does it feel to know that he's watching *you* give your offering? What does our giving have to do with our faith?

◆ The widow gave all she had as her offering to God, even though it was a tiny amount. How is our offering a sacrifice? Why isn't the amount as important as how we give?

◆ Jesus praised the woman to the disciples, but didn't tell her. Why do you think he didn't praise her face to face? What do you think happened to the widow next?

Topical Tie-Ins: Giving, Sacrifice, Faith

Extreme Life Makeover

The Scene: a live television show at Martha's house

The Simple Setup: You'll need pillows on the floor for Jesus and Mary to sit on, a space for the "studio audience" to gather on the floor, and a tray with food or dishes for Martha to carry.

For Extra Impact: Make three cue cards for the narrator to hold up to the audience. The first card should say "Clap and Cheer"; the second, "Yes! Yes! Yes!"; and the third, "Jesus! Jesus! Jesus!" Consider using simple Bible costumes.

Bible Story
Mary and Martha

Scripture
Luke 10:38-42

The Characters

Narrator: an outgoing television show host, guy or girl

Mary: a girl

Martha: a girl willing to act nervous and frazzled

Jesus: a guy

Audience: kids willing to clap and cheer

The Skit

After choosing an energetic girl for the role of Martha, cast the roles of Jesus and Mary. Ask the remaining kids to be the studio audience. If your group is particularly exuberant, establish a hand signal for the Narrator to use when it's time to cut off audience cheering.

As the skit begins, the audience is seated on the floor, center stage. The Narrator stands center stage. Jesus and Mary are seated on pillows on the floor, stage left. Martha is offstage, stage right. Lower the volume of the theme music after the introduction so the actors can be heard.

Start the "Mary and Martha" track on *The Humongous Book of Bible Skits for Children's Ministry* CD (track 35). Set your CD player on "repeat" so the track repeats.

Narrator: Welcome to Extreme Life Makeover! We're at the home of Martha, and we're broadcasting LIVE! Let's give it up for MARY AND MARTHA!

Audience: *(Claps and cheers.)*

Narrator: Mary is seated there at the feet of Jesus—wave at the audience, Mary—and Martha is…well, Martha is out back in the kitchen. We talked with our hosts before we went on the air, and here's something Martha may not know. (*Calling offstage right*) Martha, Mary thinks you need an Extreme Life Makeover!

(*Martha enters from stage right.*)

Martha: (*To Mary*) What? You don't think I'm ATTRACTIVE?

Mary: No. I mean, YES!

Martha: Well, which IS it?

Mary: You look great. That's not what I meant!

Martha: You mean I *don't* look great? Hey, Sissy, there are LOTS of guys who think I'M the attractive sister in this family!

Narrator: Before these two sisters get in a fight, let me explain. Mary thinks Martha needs an Extreme Life Makeover on the INSIDE. And once Martha changes on the inside, EVERYTHING will change!

Martha: What's wrong with my insides? My HEART feels fine. My LIVER is working. At least I THINK it is. WHAT'S WRONG WITH MY LIVER? WHY DIDN'T ANYONE TELL ME I WAS SICK?

Narrator: Relax, Martha. You're not sick. Wow, Mary, I'm starting to see what you mean. She IS a little tense, isn't she?

Martha: (*In a panic*) Tense? Why would I be TENSE? I mean, just because Jesus is here visiting at OUR house! And just because we have about a THOUSAND guests to feed and a TON of food to prepare and a MIL-LION dishes to wash! WHY WOULD I BE TENSE?

Narrator: Let's see what our studio audience has to say. Do you think Martha might need to change at least a little bit on the inside?

Audience: Yes, yes, yes!

Narrator: There you have it, Martha. The audience doesn't lie.

Martha: Well, I don't know about THAT! I only know I have a HUGE dinner to prepare and I don't have TIME for this. That lamb in the kitchen won't roast ITSELF, will it?

Mary: But, Martha, you've got to just RELAX. You're MISSING the point! JESUS is here. Don't you want to hear what he has to SAY?

Martha: Of COURSE I do! Jesus is more important than ANYTHING, but SOMEBODY'S got to cook! YOU'RE obviously not going to!

Narrator: Let's ask the audience again. Audience, should Martha cook or listen to Jesus?

Audience: Jesus, Jesus, Jesus!

Narrator: You see? There you HAVE it! They think you should sit and listen to Jesus, too!

Martha: It doesn't matter what THEY say! There is only ONE person who matters here. I'm doing this for HIM! What will Jesus EAT if I don't cook? Let's ask HIM! Jesus, it's not fair that I'm doing all the work. PLEASE tell my sister to come and help me!

Jesus: Martha, there is really only one important thing here. Mary has discovered it, sitting right here with me. I'm NOT going to take that away from her!

Narrator: You SEE, Martha? You DO need an Extreme Life Makeover—from the inside out. There's NOTHING more important than growing in your relationship with Jesus. DINNER isn't more important, and neither is sweeping out the LIVING ROOM. Well, that's our show for today! Join us next time on Extreme Life Makeover and maybe *you* can change from the inside out, too! Let's give it up for today's guests, Martha and Mary!

Audience: (*Claps and cheers.*)

Martha: You DO think I'm attractive, right?

Mary: You're the BEST, sister!

To Talk About

◆ Why do you think Martha was so worried about preparing dinner? Have you ever been nervous or worried about something? How did you handle it?

◆ Jesus said that Mary chose the most important thing. Does that mean we should never help anyone, or does it mean that we should always put Jesus first in our lives? How can you put Jesus first this week?

◆ What are things you spend your time doing instead of getting to know Jesus better?

Topical Tie-Ins: Priorities, Anxiety, Growing Closer to Jesus

Jesus Visits a Short, Mean Guy

Bible Story
Zacchaeus

Scripture
Luke 19:1-10

The Scene: a city street in Jericho

The Simple Setup: Put a chair on the left side of the stage for Zacchaeus to stand on when he's in the tree. Place two chairs facing each other stage right.

For Extra Impact: Give the crowd paper coins or play money to hand to the tax collectors.

The Characters

Narrator: a friendly storyteller
Zacchaeus: a guy
Jesus: a guy
Crowd: kids present at Zacchaeus' meeting with Jesus

Tax Collectors: two or three kids who will take money from the Crowd

The Skit

Assign the roles of Zacchaeus and Jesus. Then form the rest of the children into two groups: the Crowd and the Tax Collectors. If you have a small class, have the same child or children play the Crowd and the Tax Collectors.

As the skit begins, the Crowd is center stage. Zacchaeus and the other Tax Collectors will mingle with the Crowd. Jesus is off stage left.

Start the "Zacchaeus" track on *The Humongous Book of Bible Skits for Children's Ministry* **CD (track 36). Set your CD player on "repeat" so the track repeats.**

Narrator: It was tax time in the city of Jericho, and NO one was happy about it. Well, no one except the TAX Collectors. The Tax Collectors always took too much money from people. (*Sighs.*) It wasn't fair. Just between you and me, I think the Tax Collectors didn't give EVERYTHING they collected to the government. I think they used the REST to buy stuff for themselves. And they didn't have very good manners, either. Look at how the Tax Collectors are DEMANDING money from people in the Crowd.

(Tax Collectors approach the Crowd and ask for money.)

Narrator: There was one Tax Collector who was ESPECIALLY mean. His name was Zacchaeus.

Zacchaeus: YOU look rich. How much money do you HAVE? Give me HALF of it. NOW!

Narrator: The Crowd was upset. They HATED being robbed by Tax Collectors, but what could they do? If people DIDN'T pay taxes, the Romans came and threw the people in jail. But suddenly, the mood of the crowd changed. People were SMILING. That's because they heard that Jesus was coming to Jericho! Everyone was VERY excited.

Crowd: Yea!

Narrator: Even Zacchaeus wanted to see Jesus. But there was one SMALL problem…

(Jesus enters stage left and waves at the crowd. The crowd stands on tiptoe to see Jesus. Zacchaeus is at the back of the crowd and can't see. He tries to peek over the crowd, but can't catch a glimpse of Jesus.)

Zacchaeus: I'm TOO SHORT! Aw, man! Bummer!

Narrator: Then Zacchaeus had a GREAT idea! He could climb a tree and see OVER the crowd! He glanced around.

Zacchaeus: Which tree should I CLIMB? The pine tree over there looks easy to climb, but it's all prickly. The palm tree across the street is tall, but its branches are WAY too high. Oh, here's a SYCAMORE tree. I'll try THAT. *(Zacchaeus stands on the chair.)* Wow! I can see all the BALD spots on people's heads from up here! We should TAX bald spots. And that guy over there forgot to comb his hair this morning. We should tax BAD HAIR DAYS, too. And hey—I can see where people are hiding their coin purses. Hmm. Now why was I up here again? Oh yeah! I can see JESUS from up here! Cool!

Narrator: Jesus was waving and giving people high fives when he saw Zacchaeus climb the tree. He walked over to where Zacchaeus was hanging from the tree.

Jesus: Zacchaeus! Stop looking at people's bald spots and finding their hidden coin purses, and come down from that tree! I'm going to YOUR house today for dinner!

(Zacchaeus climbs down from the tree.)

Zacchaeus: To MY house? But I didn't even INVITE you. Wait a minute! How did you know my NAME? And how did you know what I was doing in the TREE? Are you working for the Romans?

Narrator: The Crowd was surprised that Jesus would choose to go to Zacchaeus' house, since Zacchaeus was such a MEAN Tax Collector. Hear how the Crowd is mumbling and grumbling? And see how they're POINTING at Zacchaeus? They can't BELIEVE that Jesus would spend time with a SINNER like Zacchaeus!

Zacchaeus: Are you SURE you want to hang out with me? You DO know what I do for a living, right?

Jesus: I know who you are. I know what you've done. But I STILL love you, Zacchaeus. I want to visit with you.

Zacchaeus: Sounds great, Jesus. See you there! You like lamb chops?

Narrator: Zacchaeus dashed home. He quickly called up some of his Tax Collector buddies to join him for dinner.

Zacchaeus: *(Pretending to be on the phone)* Yeah, Antonio? How about stopping by the house for dinner? I've got Jesus here. Yup—THAT Jesus. No, I DON'T know if he's going to be doing any miracles, but who knows? You can come? Great! Bring Frank and the rest of the guys.

Narrator: Zacchaeus quickly swept the floor. He washed the dishes. He took the trash outside and threw it in the trash can. He freshened up the outhouse.

(Zacchaeus and Jesus sit together in the chairs at stage right.)

Narrator: Zacchaeus had a change of heart when he met Jesus. Zacchaeus realized he'd been wrong toward people, so he returned everything he'd taken from them. Not only did he return the money he took; he gave back even more than he'd taken in the FIRST place!

Crowd: (*Cheers.*) Yea!

To Talk About

◆ The crowd felt that it was unfair Jesus ate with Zacchaeus. Tell about a time you felt something was unfair.

◆ Jesus forgave Zacchaeus. He also forgives us when we change our hearts and follow him. Tell about a time you asked Jesus for forgiveness.

◆ Zacchaeus chose to give back the money he had taken from the crowd. What's something you can do to repay someone you've wronged?

Topical Tie-Ins: Sharing, Forgiveness

Seeds, Seeds, and a few More Seeds!

Bible Story
Parable of the Sower

Scripture
Matthew 13:1-23

The Scene: a field

The Simple Setup: The stage is empty except for a chair at center stage. The farmer has a small bag of dried beans.

For Extra Impact: Give the farmer a hat and overalls.

The Characters

Narrator: a friendly storyteller

Jesus: a guy—and a very strong reader

Farmer: a guy or girl

Plants: kids willing to act like plants as they're described

Thorns: kids willing to "choke" the plants

Crowd: kids willing to sit and listen to Jesus

The Skit

After you've assigned the roles of Jesus, Farmer, and Plants, cast the rest of the children as Thorns or the Crowd. If you have just a few children, let the same children play the roles of the Crowd and Thorns.

As the skit begins, Jesus is center stage, facing stage left. Jesus sits in a chair. The Crowd is seated on the floor, stage left. The Plants, Thorns, and Farmer are at stage right where the Farmer is standing and the Plants and Thorns are seated.

Start the "Parable of the Sower" track on *The Humongous Book of Bible Skits for Children's Ministry* CD (track 37). Set your CD player on "repeat" so the track repeats.

Narrator: One day, so MANY people had come to be with Jesus that he needed to find a way to be heard by everyone. He was near a lake, so Jesus got in a boat and sat in it while the Crowd was on the shore. Jesus told them many things in PARABLES—stories that have a meaning. Here's one of the parables he shared. It seems there once was a FARMER...

Farmer: HOWDY, folks!

Jesus: This Farmer did what most farmers do: He planted some seeds. First he tossed some seeds on the path that he walked every day as he was going to his fields. See the Farmer tossing a few of the seeds on the path?

Farmer: When these seeds grow into plants, it will be REALLY easy to harvest the grain. Why, it'll already be here on the PATH. I won't even have to get my FEET dirty!

Crowd: GOOD idea!

Jesus: But the dirt on the path was hard because it had been walked on. And it was smooth, so it was easy for birds to eat the seeds.

Farmer: Hmm…THAT didn't work very well. I'd better scatter these seeds somewhere ELSE. I'll toss some seeds over THERE.

Jesus: Some of the seeds fell on ROCKY soil. The seeds grew up very quickly. See how the seeds are sprouting, lifting their faces toward the sun?

Farmer: Boy, what a CROP I'm going to get! Those plants are sprouting VERY nicely! I didn't really expect it to go so WELL, considering that the soil is shallow over there among the rocks.

Jesus: But because there wasn't much soil, when the sun came out the heat burned up the plants and they died. See them wither and die?

Crowd: Awwwwww…POOR PLANTS.

Jesus: Some of the Farmer's seeds fell near thorns. See how the Plants are growing, getting taller? They're HAPPY plants…

Crowd: *(Happily)* Happy!

Jesus: Happy RIGHT up to the moment the Thorns choked the plants, causing the plants to die. *(Thorns choke plants.)*

Crowd: *(Sad)* NOT so happy.

Jesus: But, some of the Farmer's seeds fell onto the good soil.

Crowd: Oooooooohhhh!

Jesus: The seeds grew into beautiful plants…

Crowd: Aaaaaaaawwwww!

Jesus: More plants grew than the Farmer had even imagined would grow. See them growing? And NO THORNS!

Farmer: I've never SEEN so many plants. And they're so BEAUTIFUL!

narrator: People in the Crowd nodded their heads. They understood the meaning in this story.

Crowd: Excuse us.

Jesus: Yes?

Crowd: Just in case…

Jesus: I'll explain. Many people will HEAR about the kingdom of God, but some people will not UNDERSTAND it. When that happens the enemy comes and snatches them away, just like the birds snatched the seeds along the path.

Crowd: Uh-huh.

Jesus: OTHER people will hear God's words and it will make them feel good. But then, when bad things happen in their lives, they'll forget what they heard. THESE people are like the seeds that fell on rocky soil. They grew quickly, but they withered and died when the heat of the sun beat down on them.

Crowd: Uh-huh.

Jesus: Still OTHER people heard God's words and start growing and living their lives the way God wants them to. But when bad times came, they began to worry and forgot to live God's way. These people were like the seeds that grow near thorns. The thorns choke them to death.

Crowd: Uh-huh.

Jesus: Then there are the people who hear God's words and understand how God wants them to live. They live that way. They tell others about God's words, so others can grow. These people are like seeds that grow in the good soil and bring a great harvest. Do you want to be like seeds on the path?

Crowd: (*Shaking heads*) No.

Jesus:	Do you want to be like the seeds that fell on rocky soil?
Crowd:	*(Shaking heads)* No.
Jesus:	Do you want to be like the seeds that fell among thorns?
Crowd:	*(Shaking heads)* No.
Jesus:	Do you want to be like the seeds that fell on GOOD soil?
Crowd:	*(Celebrating)* UH-HUH!

To Talk About

◆ Tell about a time you knew God's Word said to do one thing yet you chose to do something different. What happened when you chose not to obey God's Word?

◆ What are things about God that you don't understand? Who are some people who could help you understand God better?

◆ Describe a time you told someone else about your friendship with God. What was the hardest part about sharing? What was the easiest part?

Topical Tie-Ins: Listening, Obeying God, Sharing Your Faith

Welcome to the Neighborhood

The Scene: a road

The Simple Setup: You'll need no furniture on the stage. An open area works best.

For Extra Impact: Use masking tape to make a wide, winding road on the floor. Crumple brown paper grocery bags to place along the road as rocks.

Bible Story
Parable of the
Good Samaritan

Scripture
Luke 10:25-37

The Characters

Narrator: a friendly storyteller
Priest: a guy or a girl
Temple Assistant: a guy or girl
Samaritan: a guy
Jewish Man: a guy

Robbers: guys or girls willing to *pretend* to beat someone up
Patrons of the Inn: guys or girls willing to look amazed

The Skit

After you've assigned the roles of Priest, Temple Assistant, Samaritan, and Jewish Man, let the rest of your children be either the Robbers and/or the Patrons at the Inn. If you have a small group, let the same children play the part of the Robbers and Patrons of the Inn.

As the skit begins, center stage is empty. The Jewish Man is stage right, the Robbers stage left, and the Patrons of the Inn stage left. The Narrator may be offstage or at one side of the stage throughout the skit.

Narrator: One day, while Jesus was teaching about loving our neighbors, a man asked Jesus to explain something. The man wanted to know who our neighbors actually ARE. Did Jesus mean next-DOOR neighbors? people in our KNITTING CLUBS? people who have the LOCKER above ours at school? people who aren't even NICE to us? Jesus answered by telling a story.

Start the "Parable of the Good Samaritan" track on *The Humongous Book of Bible Skits for Children's Ministry* **CD (track 38). Set your CD player on "repeat" so the track repeats.**

Narrator: A Jewish Man was walking down a road. See him hiking along there, WHISTLING as he walks? Not a care in the world. Suddenly, a gang of ROBBERS jumped out at him. They pointed to the man's coin purse, so the Jewish Man wisely handed over all his money. Then the Robbers pointed at the Jewish Man's new SANDALS. So the man took off his shoes and gave them over to the Robbers. Then, the Robbers decided they wanted EVERYTHING the man had on him. So the Robbers started shoving and HITTING the Jewish Man. They knocked him to the GROUND and kicked him hard in the head and ribs. They took what they wanted and walked away. They left the Jewish Man lying in the middle of the road, half dead. A little while later, a PRIEST came walking down the same road.

Priest: My, my, what a NICE day for a walk. I LOVE to take walks. I ESPECIALLY love it when the WEATHER is nice, and the VIEW is nice, and the people I MEET are nice, and…oh, my!

Narrator: The priest saw the broken and bloodied Jewish Man lying in the road.

Priest: What IS that in the road up ahead? Looks like a big lump of something BRUISED. Eeeeyew, it's a PERSON! And it looks like this person got beat up and left here to DIE. How DISGUSTING! Well, I'm not going to get involved. I'm a PRIEST, after all. I'll just step over to the other side of the road, keep on going, and think NICE thoughts.

Narrator: So the Priest walked right on by. Then along came a Temple Assistant. He was walking FAST because he was VERY busy. Temple Assistants don't have time for stopping to admire the view. Suddenly, the Temple Assistant STOPPED. He saw the Jewish Man, who was MOANING and GROANING.

Temple Assistant: Well, THAT guy should have been more careful! Can't stop to help right now, though—gotta keep MOVING! Besides, those ROBBERS could still be around!

Narrator: So the Temple Assistant quickly walked past. Just then a SAMARITAN came walking down the road. Keep in mind the Jews HATED Samaritans. They thought Samaritans were the lowest of the LOW. NO respectable Jew wanted ANYTHING to do with a Samaritan.

Samaritan: Boy, I HATE walking on this road. I hope I don't meet any Jews. They always SCOWL at me and treat me like I'm something they scraped off the bottom of their SANDALS. So far, so good, though. I hope I…

Narrator: The Samaritan saw the wounded Jewish Man lying in the road.

Samaritan: Hey…something—or SOMEONE—is lying in the road up ahead! It looks like a man. A JEW by the looks of his clothes. Looks like some ROBBERS got ahold of him. They sure messed him up—a broken nose, black eyes, blood all over…The poor guy. He might DIE if I don't do something. I can't just walk BY. I have to HELP!

Narrator: So the Samaritan washed the Jewish Man's wounds and bandaged him. The Samaritan put the Jewish Man on his donkey and took the injured man to an inn. There, he helped the Jewish Man into a bed and took care of him. The other Patrons of the Inn were AMAZED to see a Samaritan helping a Jew. They POINTED, and whispered to each other, and RUBBED THEIR EYES as if they couldn't BELIEVE what they were seeing. But it was TRUE—a Samaritan was helping a Jew! The next day, the Samaritan gave the innkeeper two silver coins to care for the Jewish Man. That was a lot of money. And the Samaritan said he'd pay more if it cost more to care for the Jewish Man. After telling the story, Jesus asked who was a neighbor to the man who was attacked. Who do *you* think was the neighbor?

To Talk About

◆ **The Priest and the Temple assistant didn't help the wounded man. Has there ever been a time you *could* have helped someone but didn't do it? What happened?**

◆ **The Samaritans were looked down on in Bible times. Is there someone in your school or neighborhood who everyone looks down on? What could you do to treat that person better?**

◆ **Why do you think Jesus told this story? What did you learn from it?**

Topical Tie-Ins: Prejudice, Serving Others

Guest of Honor

Bible Story
Parable of the
Prodigal Son

Scripture
Luke 15:11-32

The Scene: a barnyard

The Simple Setup: You will need no furniture on the stage; an open area where it's easy for your "animals" to move around is best.

For Extra Impact: Provide oversize bib overalls and hats to children playing human roles.

The Characters

Narrator: a friendly storyteller
Fatted Calf: a guy or girl
Father: a guy
Oldest Son: a guy or girl

Youngest Son: a guy or girl
Barnyard Animals: children willing to impersonate chickens, cats, sheep, or goats

The Skit

After assigning the roles of Fatted Calf, Father, Oldest Son, and Youngest Son, form the rest of the children into four groups: chickens, cats, sheep, and goats. Consider working with the class on their animal imitations before the skit begins. If you have just a few children, let the same children play all the barnyard animal parts.

As the skit begins, the Youngest Son and Father are stage left. The animals are center stage. The Oldest Son is offstage, stage right. The Narrator may be offstage or at the edge of the stage.

Start the "Parable of the Prodigal Son" track on *The Humongous Book of Bible Skits for Children's Ministry* CD (track 39). Set your CD player on "repeat" so the track repeats.

Narrator: Our skit opens in a barnyard. Maybe you haven't BEEN in a barnyard lately, so let me describe it. The FIRST thing you need to know is that THIS barnyard isn't like the ones you see in picture books. It's DIRTY, with LOTS of animals wandering around bumping into each other and looking for food. See the animals wandering around? They all get along pretty well, even the CATS (*pause for cats to meow*) and the CHICKENS (*pause for chickens to cluck*). The sheep (*pause for sheep to bleat*) and goats (*pause for goats to bleat*) smile at each other, too. And that's the SECOND thing you should know about this barnyard: It's a very FRIENDLY place. EVERYONE here is happy. Well…ALMOST everyone. The FATTED CALF is a little NERVOUS.

Fatted Calf: I got a BAD feeling about this…My job as a fatted calf is pretty sweet. I do whatever I want. Eat, sleep, and be merry—that's MY deal. The only hard part of the job is having everyone call me "FATTED." I think of myself as the "Pleasantly PLUMP Calf," but that name hasn't caught on yet. Usually everything is CALM, but it feels like SOME-THING is up. Everyone has been coming around LOOKING at me, and I don't know WHY.

Narrator: It's been an EXCITING few days around the farm. The farmer's YOUNGEST SON, who left town MONTHS ago, has come home. The cats (*pause*) were glad to see him—he always petted them. The sheep (*pause*) think he's a great guy, too. The Fatted Calf…

Fatted Calf: Hey—Pleasantly PLUMP Calf!

Narrator: Sorry. The Pleasantly PLUMP Calf doesn't care one way or the other. But the goats (*pause*) aren't so sure—he always ignored them. And all the animals remember how horrible the scene was when the Youngest Son LEFT. All the animals watched as the Farmer and his Youngest Son talked…

Youngest Son: (*Walking back and forth, arguing with Father*) But Dad, it's just not FAIR! I slave and SLAVE for you on this farm, and what do I get in return? NOTHING! I need room to grow into the person I was MEANT to be! I need some FREEDOM.

Father: (*Concerned for his son*) Freedom? You want FREEDOM? You HAVE it! Because we work the land, you've got freedom from HUNGER! You've got freedom from the WEATHER here in our nice house! You've got RESPONSIBILITY, and pride in a job well done. And ONE of these days, this whole FARM will be split between you and your older brother. What more could you ASK?

Youngest Son: I could ask for THIS: Give me MY share of the farm NOW!

Father: But, Son…that's like wishing I was DEAD.

Youngest Son: Dad, I need to go find myself. And I won't find myself on this STINK-ING FARM! If you love me, give me the cash and I'm OUTTA here!

Narrator: They argued back and forth until the Father finally let his Young-est Son go. The kid was whistling as he packed up his donkey and headed out. He had BIG plans in BIG places. The animals didn't know where he was going, but they knew the Father was worried. So they said their goodbyes in their own special ways. The sheep bleated. (*Pause.*) The GOATS bleated. (*Pause.*) The CATS meowed. (*Pause.*) And the Pleasantly Plump CALF hardly noticed.

Fatted Calf: Yeah, WHATEVER. Send a postcard.

(*Youngest Son exits stage right.*)

Narrator: Every day, the Father stood outside his house and looked down the road. He just STARED. He'd say things like:

Father: My SON, my son.

Narrator: Then he'd hang his head. That Youngest Son just about broke his Father's HEART. Then one morning—the Youngest Son was BACK.

Fatted Calf: So did he strike it RICH? Did he come back to BRAG to his big brother?

Narrator: Not exactly. He'd lost every penny of his inheritance. He'd partied like there was no tomorrow, and one day he woke up and there WAS no tomorrow—at least as far as his MONEY went. He was FLAT BROKE. He'd been working at a PIG farm for food and a place to sleep. He was STARVING to death!

Fatted Calf: A PIG farm? A nice Jewish boy doesn't belong in a job like THAT.

Narrator: That's what he finally decided. THAT'S why he came home.

Fatted Calf: Wow…Did his Father take him back? There's no way I'D do that!

Narrator: Good thing you aren't the Father, then. He gave his Youngest Son a new ring and a new robe, and they're going to have a PARTY, too.

Fatted Calf: A PARTY? Cool! You want to have a PARTY, chickens? *(Pause.)* How about YOU, sheep? *(Pause.)* And YOU, goats? *(Pause.)* And I KNOW you're party ANIMALS, you kitties! *(Pause.)*

Narrator: Everyone seems happy about the Youngest Son except for the Oldest Son. He found his Father and said…

Oldest Son: I can't BELIEVE this! He takes your MONEY…he THROWS the money away on loose living…and you WELCOME HIM BACK? I hate to say it, but my little brother is a BUM!

Father: Son, I understand you're angry…

Oldest Son: Angry? I'm FURIOUS! I work on this farm my entire LIFE, and what do I get? NOTHING! My little brother gets a PARTY! What's with THAT?

Father: Your brother isn't getting a party because of what he did. He's getting a party because he's ALIVE. It was like he was DEAD to me, and now he's BACK. You've ALWAYS been with me, Son. Everything I HAVE is yours. Can't you just be happy your brother is HOME?

Fatted Calf: The Oldest Son should just lighten up, you know? Have the party. Relax. Have a good time. Eat up. You know what? I'VE been invited!

Narrator: You? Yeah, I've heard that…

Fatted Calf: In fact, I'm gonna be the GUEST OF HONOR! Isn't THAT cool?

 To Talk About

◆ **Which character in our skit do you feel is most like you?**

◆ **The father in our skit forgave his son. How does it feel to think that God is willing to forgive you of your sins, too?**

◆ **Describe a time that your actions affected others in ways you didn't expect. What happened?**

Topical Tie-Ins: Family, Forgiveness, How Your Actions Affect Others

A Most Unusual Parade

Bible Story
The Triumphant Entry

Scripture
Luke 19:28-44

The Scene: outside Jerusalem

The Simple Setup: Use chair backs to make a pen for the colt on stage left; leave the rest of the stage open.

For Extra Impact: Give the Crowd old coats to place on the floor.

The Characters

Narrator: a friendly storyteller

Jesus: a guy

Interrupter: a guy or girl

Disciple 1: a guy or girl

Disciple 2: a guy or girl

Crowd: children willing to lay "cloaks" before Jesus

Pharisees: children willing to scowl

The Skit

After you've assigned the roles of Jesus, Interrupter, and Disciples, form the rest of your children into two groups: the Crowd and the Pharisees.

As the skit begins, Jesus and two of his Disciples are stage right, near a village. Narrator and Interrupter may be at one side of the stage throughout the skit. The Pharisees are at stage left.

Narrator: This is the true account of when Jesus was the star of a most UNUSUAL parade.

Interrupter: A parade? I LOVE parades! I saw a circus parade once with lions and elephants and clowns! I LOVE circus parades!

Narrator: This WASN'T a circus parade.

Interrupter: Oh! Then it must have been a HOMECOMING parade with MARCHING BANDS and FLOATS and FIRETRUCKS! The firetrucks always have their FLASHERS flashing! You can't BEAT a homecoming parade!

Narrator: No, it wasn't a homecoming parade. It was…

Interrupter: Maybe it was a PATRIOTIC parade! You know, with people sitting in cars, WAVING! I was at a patriotic parade where they threw CANDY! I LOVE candy!

Narrator: Trust me—this ISN'T a parade like you've seen before. If you'd just let me TELL you about it, you'd SEE.

Interrupter: OK. I'll just stand here.

Narrator: Thank you.

Interrupter: And I won't say ANOTHER WORD.

Narrator: Um…SURE. THIS parade was all about Jesus entering the city of Jerusalem, and it was a BIG deal. Jesus and his Disciples were walking toward the city of Jerusalem. See them there, walking along?

Interrupter: Well, I can…

Narrator: Don't feel you have to actually ANSWER these questions.

Interrupter: Oh…got it.

Narrator: Before Jesus reached Jerusalem, he asked two of his Disciples to do an important errand for him.

Disciple 1: Sure thing, Jesus! We're your guys! What is it—do you want us to scout out the PHARISEES so we know where they might AMBUSH you? Or should we go hold a PRESS CONFERENCE for you? Anything you want, Lord!

Jesus: I want you to go to the village ahead of you, and as you enter it, you will find a colt tied there.

Disciple 2: Find the colt. Got it.

Jesus: This is a colt that no one has ever ridden.

Disciple 1: Find the colt no one has RIDDEN. Got it.

Jesus: Untie the colt and bring it here. If anyone asks you, "Why are you untying it?" tell him, "The Lord needs it."

Disciple 2:   Got it. Wait a minute…you want us to go steal a DONKEY for you?

Narrator: The Disciples did as they were told, and they found the colt right where Jesus told them to look. And the owner of the colt gladly gave it to them.

Interrupter: Good thing. Donkey thieves get in a LOT of trouble.

Narrator: The Disciples brought the colt back to Jesus and put their coats on the donkey's back so it would be more comfortable to ride. As Jesus and the Disciples got nearer Jerusalem, a Crowd gathered. And the Crowd knew EXACTLY what they were seeing.

Start the "Triumphant Entry" track on _The Humongous Book of Bible Skits for Children's Ministry_ CD (track 40). Set your CD player on "repeat" so the track repeats.

Interrupter: Um…they saw Jesus on a donkey?

Narrator: True, but they ALSO remembered the prophets had said Israel's king would ride into town on a colt. They knew THIS was a sign that Jesus was their KING! The Crowd laid their coats down on the road in front of the donkey, sort of like a red carpet.

Interrupter: What a cool parade!

Narrator: Not everyone thought so. The PHARISEES saw what was happening, and THEY knew about the prophecy, too.

Interrupter: Are THOSE the Pharisees over there? The MEAN-looking guys who are SCOWLING?

Narrator: That's them.

Interrupter: The Pharisees didn't LIKE Jesus very much, did they?

Narrator: They didn't believe Jesus was God's Son. They didn't WANT Jesus to be their king. But the CROWD wanted Jesus. The Crowd started CHEERING. They started CLAPPING. They were HAPPY to see Jesus!

Interrupter: Did Jesus WAVE at the people? Did he throw CANDY?

Narrator: The Bible doesn't tell us EVERYTHING that happened, but Jesus probably didn't throw candy. We DO know he came in peace and that he came to Jerusalem to give his life for us on the cross. That's why this parade is called the TRIUMPHANT ENTRY.

To Talk About

◆ Jesus had a job for two of his disciples. What job do you think Jesus might have for you this week?

◆ Jesus' followers praised God for the miracles they'd seen. What's something Jesus has done in your life? How can you praise Jesus this week?

◆ Jesus came to Jerusalem so he could give his life for us. That's real love! How can you show Jesus' love to others?

Topical Tie-Ins: Serving Others, Praise, Jesus' Love

fabulous feet!

Bible Story
Jesus Washes the
Disciples' Feet

Scripture
John 13:1-17

The Scene: the upper room

The Simple Setup: You'll need chairs so the three Disciples, Jesus, and Peter can be seated.

For Extra Impact: Use a real bowl and towel for Jesus instead of miming it. Have Water Kids wave strips of blue crepe paper over their feet and pretend to wash them as they say the poem. Also consider having them take off their shoes.

The Characters

Disciple 1: a guy or a girl—barefoot
Disciple 2: a guy or a girl—barefoot
Disciple 3: a guy or a girl—barefoot
Jesus: a guy
Peter: a guy—barefoot

Water Kids: kids willing to repeat the washing-feet poem while Jesus washes feet, and pretend to wash their own feet. They'll also wiggle their toes and shake off dusty feet on cue.

The Skit

After you've cast the three Disciples, Jesus, and Peter, form the rest of your children into a group and teach them the simple washing-feet poem.

As the skit begins, Peter and Jesus are sitting stage left. The three Disciples are sitting at center stage. The Water Kids sit stage right, on the floor.

Disciple 1:   What a WEEK! Did you see the size of the crowds that came to Jerusalem, to celebrate the Passover? It was so cool when Jesus rode that donkey through the streets, with people waving palm branches and cheering. They all said Jesus was their king. What an exciting time! It was GREAT!

Disciple 2:   Yeah, and now we're here in this room, waiting for the Passover meal to be served. I've always loved the Passover.

Disciple 1:   Me, too. Since I was a little guy I've loved remembering how God saved his people from our enemies. It's a real blessing to spend this time with Jesus. I can't wait to get started.

Disciple 3: Yeah, but my feet are dirty.

Disciple 1: WHAT?

Disciple 3: I did a lot of walking today on dusty roads, and I'm wearing sandals. Usually a servant washes your feet before a big deal like Passover… but nobody's shown up. And my FEET are dirty!

Disciple 1: You complain too much.

(Jesus goes to first Disciple with pretend bowl and a towel.)

Disciple 1: Jesus, what are you doing?

Disciple 2: Is HE going to wash our feet?

Disciple 3: Isn't there a SERVANT to do it?

 Start the "Jesus Washes the Disciples' Feet" track on *The Humongous Book of Bible Skits for Children's Ministry* **CD (track 41). Set your CD player on "repeat" so the track repeats.**

(Jesus mimes pouring water, washing Disciple 1's feet, and wipes the feet with towel.)

Water Kids: There is Jesus washing feet,

The King is on his knees!

He's serving his disciples,

As kindly as you please!

(Disciple 1 stands when Jesus is finished.)

Disciple 1: I felt a little embarrassed when Jesus knelt and washed my dirty feet. What was he DOING? This was JESUS! We should be serving HIM! I didn't feel worthy of having Jesus wash MY feet.

(Jesus mimes pouring water, washing Disciple 2's feet, and wipes the feet with towel.)

Water Kids: There is Jesus washing feet,

The King is on his knees!

He's serving his disciples,

As kindly as you please!

(Disciple 2 stands when Jesus is finished.)

Disciple 2: I was worried Jesus wouldn't WANT to wash MY feet. I forgot to wash them this morning. They were so SMELLY. I wondered if he'd scold me or make a scrunched-up face and pass me by. I was ASHAMED. But Jesus washed them until they were SPARKLING clean.

(Jesus mimes pouring water, washing Disciple 3's feet, and wipes the feet with towel.)

Water Kids: There is Jesus washing feet,

The King is on his knees!

He's serving his disciples,

As kindly as you please!

Disciple 3: I WANTED my feet to be washed. I'm so grateful Jesus cares about me. He showed it, too, by washing the dirt off my toes. He saw what I needed, and he wasn't too proud to help me. After Jesus washed my feet, he went to Simon Peter.

Peter: Lord, are you going to wash MY feet?

Jesus: You don't understand why right now, but later you will.

Disciple 2: Peter pulled back his feet and said:

Peter: NO, you're too important to wash MY FEET.

Jesus: Unless you do it, you will have no part of me.

Disciple 3: Peter didn't like to hear that. I think it scared Peter that maybe Jesus wouldn't want him. So Peter offered even more for Jesus to wash.

Peter: Then Lord, wash my HANDS and HEAD, too!

Jesus: If you've already had a bath, then you only need to wash what's dirty, YOUR FEET!

(Jesus mimes pouring water, washing Peter's feet, and wipes the feet with towel.)

Water Kids: There is Jesus washing feet,

The King is on his knees!

He's serving his disciples,

As kindly as you please!

Jesus: Do you disciples understand WHY I did that? You call me Lord and Teacher, and that's right. Now that I've served you by washing your feet, you need to serve each OTHER. A servant isn't greater than his master. If I can serve others, so can YOU!

Peter: Jesus washed MY FEET. He got down on his knees, rolled up his sleeves, took each foot and scrubbed off all the dirt. I could hardly BELIEVE it. I couldn't understand why he'd DO that. But I get it now. If Jesus can serve others, so can I.

To Talk About

◆ **What if the leader of your country came to your house to wash your feet? That's how the disciples felt. What do you think Jesus was trying to teach them?**

◆ **The disciples probably felt humbled to have Jesus wash their feet. Describe a time when you felt humbled.**

◆ **Jesus showed us we can be a servant and help others. How do you help the people you know?**

Topical Tie-Ins: Humility, Embarrassment, Serving Others

Something Big in Jerusalem

Bible Story
The Last Supper

Scripture
Luke 22:7-23

The Scene: Jerusalem and the upper room

The Simple Setup: Stage left is Jerusalem; leave the stage open. Stage right is the upper room; place a semicircle of pillows on the floor for Jesus and the disciples. Place a tablecloth in front of the pillows and on it grape juice and bread.

For Extra Impact: If it's acceptable in your church, let the children share communion.

The Characters

Narrator: a storyteller
Jesus: a guy or girl
Peter: a guy or girl
John: a guy or girl

Crowd: kids willing to walk about making crowd noises
Disciples: kids who'll act out the actions described by the Narrator

The Skit

Select the role of Jesus carefully. Give it to someone who will play the role without hamming it up. After assigning the roles of Jesus, Peter, and John, form the remaining children in two groups: the Crowd, and the Disciples. Ask one Crowd member to carry a water pitcher.

As the skit begins, the Narrator is center stage. All actors are stage left.

Start the "Last Supper" track on *The Humongous Book of Bible Skits for Children's Ministry* CD (track 42). Set your CD player on "repeat" so the track repeats.

Narrator: It was the day of Passover, and Jesus and the Disciples were in the crowd gathering in Jerusalem. People were EVERYWHERE, preparing for the Passover celebration. See how the Crowd is rushing back and forth? First they're going left...then right...then left again...they're really moving! You can HEAR the hubbub.

Crowd: HUBBUB, HUBBUB, HUBBUB.

Narrator: And now the Crowd is just milling about. And the fact that it was the Passover wasn't lost on Jesus' disciples. Peter and John were especially curious about arrangements.

Peter: I'm telling you, we are NEVER going to get a reservation! Every place is booked SOLID! A few years back, my wife and I tried to get a place to celebrate the Passover on short notice—forget about it! You need to book ahead at LEAST six months!

John: And I'M saying I'm sure Jesus lined SOMETHING up!

Peter: Then why don't we KNOW about it? Someone should be getting things set up RIGHT NOW!

Jesus: Peter, John, would you come over here?

(Peter and John come to Jesus.)

John: See? I'll bet he's going to tell us where we're eating Passover.

Jesus: I'd like you to go fix the Passover meal.

Peter: US?

John: Have you ever TASTED Peter's cooking, Jesus?

Peter: Hey—YOU'RE the one who tried to make FISH PIE! Besides, where do we go to DO this?

Jesus: As you enter the city, a man carrying a jar of water will meet you. Follow him to the house he enters, and say to the owner of the house that the Teacher asks where the guest room is. He'll show you a large upper room, all furnished. Make preparations for the Passover there.

Peter: Um…could you cover that LAST part again?

Jesus: Last part?

Peter: Yeah—everything after we meet a guy carrying water…

John: I got it, Jesus. We're ON it.

(Peter and John move to stage left, moving through the crowd.)

Peter: Great…there must be a MILLION people here, and everyone is carrying SOMETHING. Like we're going to EVER see some guy with a jug of water!

John: I'll see him.

Peter: You? HA! You wouldn't see him if the guy was carrying a CAMEL! The streets are just too CROWDED. Why, I'll bet…

John: Hey—THERE he is! Just like Jesus SAID! Follow me!

Peter: (Grumbling) Boy, there's going to be no LIVING with John after this…

(John and Peter cross to stage right, following student with water pitcher.)

Pause the "Last Supper" track.

Narrator: Later, all the Disciples were gathered in the upper room. See how they're sitting together? Outside, the Crowds have thinned out as all over the city families and friends celebrate the Passover together.

Crowd: HUBBUB, HUBBUB, HUBBUB.

Narrator: I said the crowds had THINNED OUT! They're QUIETER than that!

Crowd: (Whispering) Hubbub. Hubbub. Hubbub.

Narrator: Better! In the upper room, JESUS was speaking.

Jesus: I've been longing to eat this meal with you before my SUFFERING begins.

Peter: Hey, this is a PARTY, right? What's with all the SUFFERING talk?

John: Shhh!

Narrator: Jesus took a cup and gave thanks. He passed the cup to one of his Disciples and said…

Jesus: Take this and divide it among you. For I tell you I will not drink again of the fruit of the vine until the kingdom of God comes.

Narrator: Then Jesus took bread, gave thanks, then broke the bread and gave it to his Disciples. Jesus said…

Jesus: This is my body, given for you. Eat it to remember me.

Narrator: The Disciples looked at each other. They all seemed to know that SOMETHING important was happening—they just weren't sure WHAT. Then Jesus said something they just couldn't BELIEVE.

Jesus: The hand of him who is going to betray me is with mine on the table.

Peter: What? BETRAY you? Who would BETRAY you?

John: Jesus, are you SURE about this?

Peter: If I catch the dirty rat who betrays you…well…it's NOT going to be pretty!

Narrator: The Disciples were SHOCKED. How could anyone at the table betray Jesus? They'd traveled together for YEARS. They'd shared meals, cried together, seen MIRACLES together…it just couldn't happen! Or could it?

To Talk About

◆ The disciples were preparing for the Passover, an important Jewish holiday. Who do you spend holidays with? How would you feel if you knew Jesus was coming to your holiday celebration?

◆ How do you think Jesus felt sharing this last supper with his disciples?

◆ Jesus knew one of his disciples (Judas) would betray him. Has one of your friends ever betrayed you? How did that feel?

Topical Tie-Ins: Friendship, Redemption, Betrayal, Family

An Arresting Development

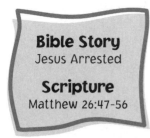

Bible Story
Jesus Arrested

Scripture
Matthew 26:47-56

The Scene: a garden at nighttime

The Simple Setup: The stage needs no furnishings. Peter will carry a cardboard tube to represent a sword.

For Extra Impact: Give the members of the crowd flashlights to hold as if they were torches. Dim room lights, and let the flashlights light the stage.

The Characters

Narrator: a warm-voiced reader

Jesus: a guy

Judas: a guy or girl who can act sinister

Peter: a guy or girl, and Peter has a *temper*

Crowd: children pretending to be an angry mob

The Skit

After you've assigned the roles of Jesus, Judas, and Peter, ask the rest of the children to play the part of the Crowd.

Jesus and Peter stand at stage right. The crowd is off stage left. The Narrator may read from offstage or on the corner of the stage.

Narrator: Kids, we're here in the middle of the night with Jesus and several of his disciples. It's been a STRANGE night. Earlier this evening, Jesus had dinner with his disciples and spent time teaching them. It was almost as if Jesus thought he wouldn't have much MORE time with them. And Judas left the room before Jesus was DONE teaching. I don't think he's up to any good. Wait, there's Judas now, coming into this quiet garden with a big Crowd.

Start the "Jesus Arrested" track on *The Humongous Book of Bible Skits for Children's Ministry* CD (track 43). Set your CD player on "repeat" so the track repeats.

Judas: Now remember the SIGNAL. The one I KISS ON THE CHEEK is the man you want.

Narrator: I KNEW it! That Judas is a SNAKE. He's going to turn Jesus over to that ANGRY crowd. Look, Judas is walking over to Jesus and giving him a kiss on the cheek.

Judas: Greetings, Teacher!

Jesus: Friend, do the job that you came to do.

Narrator: Jesus is God's Son, so he KNEW that Judas was going to double-cross him. Nothing surprises Jesus, but Jesus STILL let it HAPPEN. Listen to that angry Crowd. Do you HEAR them? They're MUTTERING threats and saying MEAN things. They want to take Jesus back to the SANHEDRIN, Jewish leaders who are going to put Jesus on TRIAL. The Sanhedrin are mad because Jesus does MIRACLES and because Jesus says he's GOD'S SON. Now look! The Crowd is rushing in! They're GRABBING Jesus! They're going to take Jesus AWAY!

Peter: NEVER! You'll NEVER take Jesus from us!

Narrator: Peter loves Jesus, and he doesn't want anyone to HURT Jesus. So Peter is drawing a sword. He's taking a swing at one of the men in the Crowd.

Peter: Take THAT!

Narrator: Peter cut off the EAR of the man! The man is yelling in pain! The man is falling to the ground, holding the side of his head!

Peter: THAT will teach you! Now, who ELSE wants to fight?

Narrator: Jesus is jumping between Peter and the Crowd. Jesus is POINTING at Peter.

Jesus: Peter, put away your sword! Don't you know that everyone who tries to solve their problems with a sword ends up being KILLED by a sword? I could call on my heavenly Father, and he'd help me! I could ask God and he'd send HUNDREDS of angels to rescue me! But If I DID that, then how would the Scriptures about me come true? Let the crowds to their work.

Narrator: Then Jesus did something AMAZING. He touched the spot on the servant's head where he used to have an ear…and his EAR GREW BACK. The CROWD stepped back. They couldn't believe their eyes. Jesus looked at the Crowd and said…

Jesus: Why are you coming to get me in the middle of the night? LOOK at all the swords and clubs you're carrying. Do you think I'm armed and dangerous? Do you think I'm going to start a fight? You could have come after me during the day when I was in the Temple courts teaching. You could have captured me THEN—but you didn't. And do you want to know WHY?

Narrator: The Crowd didn't know what to say. Jesus kept talking.

Jesus: Your taking me at night is foretold in the Scriptures. It's a prophecy that's coming true RIGHT BEFORE OUR EYES.

Narrator: Jesus was calm, but his DISCIPLES weren't. Peter and the rest of Jesus' friends ran AWAY. See them go? Jesus was left with the angry CROWD. The CROWD led Jesus out of the peaceful garden. The Crowd led Jesus to where the Sanhedrin were waiting.

To Talk About

◆ Why do you think Jesus didn't ask God to send an army of angels to rescue him? How would our lives be different if Jesus escaped from the crowd?

◆ Jesus told Peter not to solve his problems with violence. What kinds of bad things can happen to kids who use violence to solve their problems?

◆ What do you think the servant thought about Jesus after Jesus healed him? Do you think he still wanted to arrest Jesus? Why or why not? What has Jesus done for you? How do you want to respond to him?

Topical Tie-Ins: Jesus' Love, Violence, Love

He Is Risen!

The Scene: soldiers' barracks

The Simple Setup: You'll need one chair at center stage.

For Extra Impact: "Build" a simple tomb at stage right by setting two chairs about 3 feet apart, with their backs facing the audience. Drape a blanket over the chairs.

Bible Story
Jesus Resurrected

Scripture
Matthew 28:1-20

The Characters

Narrator: a friendly storyteller

Darius: a guy or girl to be a Roman soldier

Captain: a guy or girl, grumpy

Head Elder: a guy or girl

Soldier 1: a guy or girl

Soldiers: guys or girls

Elders: guys or girls

The Skit

After assigning the roles of Darius, the Captain, Soldier 1, and the Head Elder, form the rest of the children into two groups: the Soldiers and the Elders. If you have a small group, let the same children play both the Soldiers and the Elders.

As the skit begins, the Captain is seated center stage. The Soldiers are at stage left, talking and joking around. The Elders are off stage right.

Start the "Jesus Resurrected" track on *The Humongous Book of Bible Skits for Children's Ministry* **CD (track 44). Set your CD player on "repeat" so the track repeats.**

Captain:　Lieutenant Darius! Get IN here!

　　　　　　(Darius dashes in from stage left. He comes to attention and salutes.)

Darius:　I honor CAESAR! I honor ROME!

Captain:　Good for you, Lieutenant. Just tell me how your GUARD detail went last night out at Jesus' tomb.

Darius:　There were…some COMPLICATIONS, Captain.

Captain: COMPLICATIONS? How complicated can it be to guard a DEAD man? I sent you out there with the other guards because even a nitwit like YOU can't make a mistake with THIS assignment! What went WRONG?

Darius: First, let me say that it was a MOST unusual evening.

Captain: Get to the POINT, Lieutenant! I am NOT a patient man!

Soldier 1: Hey, Darius, the man you were guarding was DEAD, locked in a sealed TOMB, and you had six soldiers WITH you. How can you lose a prisoner like THAT?

(Soldiers laugh.)

Captain: YOU be quiet or you'll be cleaning out the stables for a MONTH!

Soldier 1: Sorry, Captain.

Captain: You BETTER be sorry! Still, it IS a good question. Lieutenant, the man you were guarding IS dead. He IS in a sealed tomb. You DID have six men with you. You aren't telling me you LOST Jesus' body, right?

Darius: Of COURSE not, CAPTAIN. We'd never do something like THAT!

Captain: Good. Then the body is still IN the tomb?

Darius: Um…no.

Captain: You brought it here WITH you?

Darius: Um…no. Not exactly. I think the ANGEL took it.

Captain: The ANGEL?

Darius: Right—the angel. I think the angel took it right after he rolled away the STONE from the front of the tomb.

Captain: You THINK? You aren't SURE?

Darius: No, sir. I quit looking when the men and I…um…

Captain: When you WHAT? Drew your swords and CHARGED the angel?

Darius: No, sir. When we…FAINTED.

(The soldiers all laugh again, pointing at Darius.)

Captain: QUIET—all of you!

(The soldiers quit laughing, but still snicker.)

Captain: Lieutenant, I'm giving you exactly one minute to explain—and it better be GOOD.

Darius: There was this earthquake, sir. Certainly you must have felt it down here in Jerusalem.

Captain: Yes…

Darius: Well, this angel of the Lord appeared, and he looked like lightning, and his clothes were white as snow. And he rolled the stone away from the front of the tomb.

Captain: He rolled it away by HIMSELF?

Darius: Yes, sir.

Captain: That SAME huge stone it took ALL of us to drop in place?

Darius: Yes, sir. And we all sort of passed OUT.

Captain: From FEAR? You're a ROMAN SOLDIER, Lieutenant!

Darius: Hey, Captain—it was SCARY! I went out completely, and when I was coming to I saw these two women at the tomb. They'd come looking for Jesus, and the angel told them that Jesus rose from the dead. Then I came here.

Captain: Son, I've heard about giant animals that you can ride into battle. I've heard about armies that march day after day without sleeping. But I have NEVER heard a story like YOURS. You and your men fell ASLEEP while on DUTY, didn't you?

Darius: No, SIR!

Soldier 1: That's not what I HEARD! Some of your men said you all fell ASLEEP out there!

Darius: That's NOT TRUE!

Captain: Lieutenant, I am going to have you locked away in CHAINS! Then I'm going to have you BEHEADED! Then I'm going to drag you behind my CHARIOT! Then I'm going to do it all AGAIN! Why, I…

(The Elders rush in from stage right.)

Head Elder: Captain, may we SEE you for a moment?

Captain: Well, well, well—it's the ELDERS. Aren't you supposed to be up at the TEMPLE?

Head Elder: We have a small PROBLEM.

Captain: And what's THAT? I've got problems of my OWN right now!

Head Elder: It's Jesus' body…it's GONE. We wondered if YOU had it.

Captain: Why would WE have it? I thought you and your Jewish leader buddies might have taken it.

Head Elder: Heavens, no! WE don't want anyone to think Jesus rose from the dead!

Captain: Neither do WE! We CRUCIFIED Jesus. We don't want anyone thinking he's ALIVE again! You think the disciples have Jesus' body?

Head Elder: No—because they're running around saying Jesus is ALIVE again. They're risking their LIVES doing that, and they wouldn't do it if they knew Jesus was still DEAD.

Captain: But if the disciples don't have Jesus' body, and YOU don't have it, and WE don't have it…where IS it?

Darius: Maybe it's like the angel said and Jesus is ALIVE again.

Head Elder: The thing is, that's dangerous talk. We're happy to pay you all to say that you were ASLEEP out at the tomb and the disciples stole the body.

Captain: But that's not TRUE. You said so YOURSELF!

Head Elder: Listen—we don't CARE if it's not true. It's what we want you to SAY— and we'll PAY.

Captain: Well…we don't actually make all that much money as soldiers…

Head Elder: Then it's settled. We'll get you the money right away.

Darius: There's just one other thing…

Head Elder: What?

Darius: What will you do when he shows UP again?

Head Elder: We killed him once. We can CERTAINLY kill him again.

To Talk About

◆ The news that Jesus rose from the dead changed everything for the soldiers and elders. How has the news changed your life?

◆ The elders and guards lied because they didn't want people to know that Jesus had risen from the dead. Why is it important to tell the truth about Jesus?

◆ Jesus told the disciples to tell everyone about him. Who can you tell about Jesus this week? What will you say?

Topical Tie-Ins: Faith, Worship, Obedience, Witnessing

The Rock That Rolled

Bible Story
Jesus Appears
to Mary

Scripture
John 20:1-18

The Scene: the empty tomb

The Simple Setup: You'll need a large open area. Place three chairs in a row stage left. Place a folded white cloth (such as a sheet) on the middle chair.

For Extra Impact: Drape white cloth on Jesus as a simple costume.

The Characters

Narrator: a friendly storyteller
Mary: a girl
Jesus: a guy
Peter: a guy or girl

John: a guy or girl
Angels: two boys or girls
Trees: kids willing to strike poses and move softly in the wind

The Skit

After casting the roles of Jesus, Peter, John, Mary, and the Angels, cast the rest of your children as Trees. If you have just a few children, don't cast the role of Trees or Angels.

As the skit begins, three chairs are in a row, stage left. Jesus is off stage left. The Angels will enter off stage left. Mary, John, and Peter will be off stage right. Position the Trees around the "tomb" and "garden."

Start the "Jesus Appears to Mary" track on *The Humongous Book of Bible Skits for Children's Ministry* CD (track 45). Set your CD player on "repeat" so the track repeats.

Narrator: After Jesus died on the cross, his body was placed in a tomb—a cave carved out of a hill. The tomb was in a garden. A HUGE stone was rolled in front of the tomb, and guards stood just outside to make sure NOBODY moved the stone. That tomb was sealed up TIGHT! But then, several days later, Mary Magdalene showed up in the cemetery. See her walking toward the tomb, moving between the trees?

See how SAD she is? That's because she was a follower of Jesus, and she MISSES him.

Mary: It seems so LONELY now that Jesus is gone. The disciples are all hiding out so THEY don't get arrested, too. And we all believed that Jesus was going to save our country from the Romans…I don't know what to do…

Narrator: That's when Mary looked up. She saw the tomb where Jesus was buried, but something was different. REALLY different!

Mary: The STONE! Someone has rolled the STONE away from in front of the tomb!

Narrator: Mary turned and ran back to where the disciples were gathered. She told them what she'd seen. At once Peter and John ran back to the cemetery. Here they come now, with JOHN in the lead! Man, he's fast! And now Mary is coming, too. See how they're stopping and LOOKING AROUND? John and Peter wonder if this is some sort of trap and they're going to get in TROUBLE. But it's not—and Jesus' tomb is OPEN.

John: Mary was RIGHT—the stone HAS been moved!

Mary: But who could have DONE it?

Peter: The ROMANS wouldn't have moved the stone. They want to prove Jesus is DEAD.

John: And WE didn't do it—we've been in HIDING. So how can Jesus' grave be OPEN?

Peter: I don't know…but we've got to check it out.

Narrator: Peter stooped over and went into the cave where Jesus' body had been buried. He saw the CLOTH that had been wrapped around Jesus' dead body. The cloth was folded up neatly. JOHN came into the tomb, too. The two men left the cave and went back to their homes. But Mary STAYED outside the tomb. She fell to her knees. She was CRYING.

Mary: This is so SAD!

Narrator: When Mary looked into the tomb again, she saw two angels sitting on the place where Jesus' body had been laid. The angels looked at Mary. One angel said, "Woman, why are you crying?"

Mary:	They've taken my LORD away. And I don't know where they've PUT him!
Narrator:	Mary got up and turned, and behind her was Jesus. Mary looked at him, but didn't know who he was. Jesus said…
Jesus:	Woman, why are you crying? Who is it you're looking for?
Narrator:	Mary thought the man must be the gardener who took care of the cemetery. She said…
Mary:	Sir, if you've carried him away, tell me where you put him. I'll go get him.
Narrator:	Then Jesus said Mary's name.
Jesus:	Mary.
Narrator:	That did it—Mary immediately knew who the man was. She knew he was Jesus and that Jesus had risen from the dead! Jesus told Mary not to touch him—he hadn't yet returned to God. And Jesus gave Mary a job.
Jesus:	Go tell my brothers.
Narrator:	That's just what Mary did. She ran from the garden so she could give the disciples the good news: Jesus was alive!

 ## To Talk About

◆ How do you think the disciples felt after Jesus died? Have you ever felt scared or lonely? What did you do? What made you feel better?

◆ How do you think Mary felt when she discovered that Jesus was alive? What would you do if you were the first person to learn that Jesus was alive? Who would you tell?

◆ Why is it important for us to give people the good news that Jesus is alive today? How can we share that news with others? Who could you tell that Jesus is alive?

Topical Tie-Ins: Resurrection, Discouragement, Hope, Witnessing

Three's Company!

The Scene: outdoors

The Simple Setup: Large open stage or long aisle. About midway on the road, drape a piece of gray or brown cloth over a low stool to make a *rock* for one of the characters to sit on.

For Extra Impact: Create a *flash* of light off stage when the Narrator mentions Jesus appearing and disappearing.

Bible Story
Walk to Emmaus

Scripture
Luke 24:13-35

The Characters

Narrator: a friendly storyteller
Believer 1: a guy or girl
Believer 2: a guy or girl
Jesus: a guy

Other Travelers: children willing to walk back and forth, sometimes doing activities suggested by the Narrator

The Skit

After assigning the roles of Jesus, Believer 1, and Believer 2, cast the rest of the children in the role of Other Travelers.

As the skit begins, two men walk slowly down a road. They are joined by a third man. Other Travelers are also walking back and forth on the path.

Start the "Walk to Emmaus" track on *The Humongous Book of Bible Skits for Children's Ministry* CD (track 46). Set your CD player on "repeat" so the track repeats.

Narrator: Just after Jesus rose from the dead, two Believers were walking along a road between Jerusalem and the town of Emmaus. They trudged along slowly because they were SAD. See how they're just POKING along? Those are two DEPRESSED hikers!

Believer 1: It's just SO sad. I thought Jesus was going to be our KING.

Believer 2: Same here. I figured he'd be up on a THRONE, not on a CROSS.

Narrator: The two Believers were so busy talking that they hardly noticed when ANOTHER man walked up behind them. The third man was JESUS, but the Believers didn't RECOGNIZE him.

Jesus: Mind if I join you? We seem to be going the same direction.

Believer 1: Suit yourself, buddy, but we may not be very good COMPANY.

Jesus: I can see you're feeling glum. Why IS that?

Believer 1: Man, you must be the only person in all of JERUSALEM who hasn't heard the news!

Believer 2: YEAH! The whole town is buzzing about the TERRIBLE things that happened there last week.

Jesus: Really? WHAT things?

Believer 1: Things that happened to JESUS, the man from NAZARETH.

Believer 2: He was a PROPHET, you know, and he did wonderful MIRACLES.

Believer 1: AND he was a mighty TEACHER. He was highly respected by God AND man.

Jesus: Tell me about it.

Narrator: As they walked, they passed Other Travelers. But the two Believers didn't even NOTICE when the Other Travelers nodded a polite hello. The two Believers didn't notice when Other Travelers WAVED. The two Believers didn't notice when the Other Travelers did little TAP DANCES. The three men kept talking while the Other Travelers passed to and fro.

Believer 1: Jesus did GOOD things for people, like healing the sick and preaching about how much God LOVES us. But the religious leaders in Jerusalem had Jesus ARRESTED.

Believer 2: Then they handed Jesus over to the Romans. THOSE are some pretty tough guys. You don't want to mess with THEM!

Narrator: The three men kept talking, even though the Other Travelers stopped and did five jumping jacks each.

Believer 1: The Romans KILLED Jesus. They nailed him to a cross.

Believer 2: (Shaking head) We thought he was the MESSIAH and that he came to rescue our people, but you can't lead an army when you're nailed to a cross.

Believer 1: After they killed Jesus, they put his body in a tomb. That was three days ago.

Believer 2: And this morning some women from our group said that when they went to Jesus' tomb, it was EMPTY.

Believer 1: Yeah—they said there were angels. And when some men we know checked it out, THEY said Jesus' body was gone, too. We just can't figure it out…

Jesus: What is the matter with you foolish men?

Believer 2: Hey, buddy—no need to call us NAMES!

Jesus: ALL of this was written in the Scriptures. It says the MESSIAH would have to experience some very hard things before he was done here on earth!

Narrator: As they kept walking, Jesus quoted Scripture and explained what the Scriptures said about himself. But the two Believers still didn't recognize Jesus. It was getting late, so the two Believers invited Jesus to stay with them. And Jesus agreed—see Jesus NODDING?

(The two Believers and Jesus stop at stage right.)

When it was time for the evening meal, Jesus sat down with them and asked a blessing on the food. Then Jesus took a small loaf of BREAD, broke it, and passed it to the two Believers. Suddenly the two Believers RECOGNIZED Jesus. Their eyes BUGGED OUT Their jaws DROPPED! And Jesus DISAPPEARED.

Believer 1: That was HIM! That was JESUS!

Believer 2: I knew SOMETHING was strange! I had this strange, TINGLY feeling back when he was talking about the Scriptures!

Believer 1: We've got to get back to JERUSALEM! We've got to let the other believers know about this! JESUS IS ALIVE!

Believer 2: But what about DINNER? I'm HUNGRY!

Believer 1: Dinner can wait! Come ON!

Narrator: The two Believers ran back to Jerusalem. They didn't slow down when they passed Other Travelers. The Other Travelers stood off the path because the two Believers were moving so FAST. When the two Believers reached Jerusalem, they proclaimed it far and wide: THE LORD IS ALIVE!

Believer 1 & 2: THE LORD IS ALIVE!

 To Talk About

◆ The two believers were sad. When are times in your life when you're sad?

◆ Why do you think the two believers didn't recognize Jesus? How do you think they felt when they realized Jesus was alive?

◆ Why do you think Jesus called the two believers "foolish"? Could he call us "foolish" for the same reasons?

Topical Tie-Ins: Sadness, Crucifixion, Jesus' Resurrection

Double Dose of Doubt

The Scene: locked room

The Simple Setup: No furniture or props are needed; just an empty stage.

For Extra Impact: Have children wear robes or other Bible-time costuming.

Bible Story
Jesus Appears to Thomas

Scripture
John 20:24-31

The Characters

Narrator: an expressive storyteller
Thomas: a guy or girl
Jesus: a guy
Peter: a guy or girl

John: a guy or girl
Disciples: a group of kids who'll obey the directions given by the Narrator

The Skit

After you've assigned the roles of Thomas, Jesus, Peter, and John, cast the remaining children in the role of Disciples.

The stage is empty until Peter and John enter stage left. Thomas and the Disciples are offstage, stage right. Jesus is offstage, stage left. Narrator is offstage or at one side of stage.

Start the "Jesus Appears to Thomas" track on *The Humongous Book of Bible Skits for Children's Ministry* CD (track 47). Set your CD player on "repeat" so the track repeats.

Peter: OK, I think we're SAFE. I didn't see anyone following us. Did YOU?

John: No—at least not any SOLDIERS. I checked the street before we closed the door, too.

Peter: The Roman patrols are in the street, and they're checking doors sometimes. Did you LOCK the door?

John: Absolutely! BOTH locks. No WAY anyone is getting in through that door—it's ROCK SOLID!

Peter: You know, it was horrible for Jesus to die like that...

John: I know. I was there.

Peter: The LORD has forgiven me for running away, but I don't know HOW long it'll be before I forgive MYSELF...

John: If JESUS forgives you, can you do any less for yourself? Listen, are the others already here? Are we the last two?

Peter: I'll find out. Hey, DISCIPLES!

(The Disciples and Thomas enter from stage right.)

John: Looks like we're all here. INCLUDING Thomas.

Thomas: It's not my fault I wasn't here for the last meeting.

Peter: You mean the one where Jesus appeared to us?

Thomas: I know you say that happened, and I WANT to believe, but I just can't.

John: WHAT was it you said? "Unless I see the nail marks in his hands and put my finger where the nails were, and put my hand into his side, I will not believe it." Your words EXACTLY, aren't they?

Peter: It really DID happen, Thomas. We ALL saw it!

(The Disciples nod their heads in agreement.)

Thomas: Listen, I know you THINK you saw Jesus. And I'm not saying you made it up. But THINK about it—you'd just lost your best friend. Jesus had just been killed on the cross.

Peter: So what?

Thomas: So you were all under a lot of STRAIN. You were STRESSED. You hadn't slept for DAYS. That's the PERFECT situation for people to start to imagine they're seeing things that really aren't there.

Peter: Meaning WHAT? You're calling us LIARS?

Thomas: No! I'm just saying that it's...it's easy to THINK you see someone when that person isn't really THERE. Like when you're out in a boat fishing and you look to shore and think you see a friend. Then you look AGAIN and it turns out your friend is just a piece of driftwood. It was an honest MISTAKE.

Peter: I think Thomas is calling us LIARS!

John: That's NOT what he's saying, Peter. But you are saying that you're not going to take our word that Jesus is alive, right?

Thomas: I was there, John. I saw his body, too. I KNOW he was buried. I KNOW he's dead.

John: And you saw the miracles he did in front of us for YEARS, Thomas. You KNOW Jesus is God's Son!

Thomas: Still…I don't want to get my HOPES up. Until I see him with my own two eyes…

Peter: AND see the nail marks. AND put your hand in his wound. We KNOW. Thomas, you're such a DOUBTER!

Thomas: Hey—explain THIS to me: How did Jesus get into a locked room?

John: We don't know.

Thomas: And how did Jesus get past all the Roman patrols?

John: We don't know THAT, either.

Thomas: Plus, there's that matter of Jesus getting out of a sealed TOMB. Bet you can't explain THAT, either!

John: Nope. I can just tell you what we saw. Jesus IS alive.

Thomas: Well, you're a LITTLE SHORT on answers! Like I said, unless I can see the nail marks…

(Jesus enters from stage left.)

Jesus: In my hands? Peace be with you. Thomas put your fingers on the marks in my hands. Touch my side. Stop doubting and BELIEVE.

Thomas: Jesus—is that…that YOU? *(Kneels.)* My Lord and my God!

(All the Disciples kneel.)

Jesus: You believe because you have seen me. Blessed are those who have NOT seen and STILL believe.

Narrator: Jesus did a many other miracles at that time, too. They're not all recorded in the Bible. But what happened here—Jesus appearing to Thomas and the other Disciples—it's written in the book of John that you, too, might believe on the Lord Jesus.

To Talk About

◆ The disciples were afraid they might be killed, like Jesus was killed. Have you ever been afraid of anything because you were following Jesus?

◆ Thomas needed to be sure about what had happened. Is it OK to have questions about God?

◆ The disciples were sad, and Jesus comforted them. How does Jesus comfort you when you're sad?

Topical Tie-Ins: Fear, Questions, Trusting God

Up, Up and Away

The Scene: Luke reads a letter to his friend "Theo."
The Simple Setup: Place a chair at stage left.
For Extra Impact: Break out the choir robes for costumes.

Bible Story
Jesus Taken to Heaven

Scripture
Acts 1:1-11

The Characters

Theo: a guy
Jesus: a guy

Angels: two guys
Disciples: guys and girls

The Skit

After you've assigned the roles of Theo and Jesus, form the rest of your children into a group of Disciples.

As the skit begins, Theo sits in a chair at stage left. The Disciples and Jesus are center stage. The Angels are off stage right.

Start the "Jesus Taken to Heaven" track on *The Humongous Book of Bible Skits for Children's Ministry* CD (track 48). Set your CD player on "repeat" so the track repeats.

Theo: *(Sitting at a table reading the script as if it were a letter)* Hi, Theo! This is Luke. In my first letter, I told you a LOT about Jesus. I told you about his TEACHING and about his MIRACLES. I told you about his SUF-FERING, too. Then I mentioned how Jesus SHOWED himself to his Disciples after Jesus rose from the dead. But now I want to tell you more about those Disciples. They had LOTS of questions for Jesus, but sometimes the Disciples didn't seem to quite get what Jesus was trying to DO. Once, they were all excited about Jesus restoring the kingdom to Israel. The Disciples were jumping up and down and they kept ask-ing the same question.

Disciples: Is it TIME yet? Is it TIME yet? Are you setting up your KINGDOM now?

Jesus: Listen, it's not for you to know, OK? Will you give it a REST? The Father will let us know when it's time!

Theo: (*Reading*) Jesus had taught the Disciples so many things. One of those things was that the Holy Spirit was going to be a BIG part of their future. But the Disciples just DIDN'T seem to get it. They had just one thing on their minds.

Disciples: Is it TIME yet? Is it TIME yet? Are you setting up your KINGDOM now?

Jesus: One more time: The Father will let us KNOW when it's time—and not one MINUTE earlier! While you're waiting, I DO have a job for you, though.

Disciples: (*Celebrating*) All RIGHT!

Jesus: You're going to be my WITNESSES! You get to tell EVERYONE all the things that I've taught you and about the ADVENTURES we've been on. I want you to bring the love of GOD to people.

Disciples: (*Raise their arms in victory.*) Yeah!

Jesus: You'll be my witnesses in JERUSALEM!

Disciples: (*Raise their arms in victory.*) Yeah!

Jesus: Those are people just like you. They're your friends and neighbors.

Disciples: (*Raise their arms in victory.*) Yeah!

Jesus: And you get to be my witnesses in all of JUDEA!

Disciples: (*Raise their arms in victory.*) Yeah!

Jesus: I thought you'd like THAT, too. You know how to get to Judea—it's close by. You'll have to do a bit of WALKING, but we can't be selfish with this good news from God.

Disciples: (*Raise their arms in victory.*) Yeah!

Jesus: And then you get to be my witnesses in SAMARIA!

Disciples: (*Raise their arms in victory.*) Yeah! (*Look at each other and then drop arms.*) No—BOOO! We mean BOOO! BOOO!

Jesus: I THOUGHT this would happen. You're good Jews, so you don't especially LIKE Samaritans. There's been bad blood between you and them for GENERATIONS. But the love of God is BIGGER than racism…and we've already covered this "love your enemy" thing. You have to tell the good news of God to EVERYONE—even people who aren't your favorite folks.

Disciples: Well…OK. We guess…

Jesus: And then…

Disciples: We're not done yet?

Jesus: Not yet. You get to be my witnesses to the VERY ENDS OF THE WORLD.

Disciples: But we don't KNOW anybody there.

Jesus: Listen: The good news from God is SO big that you've got to take it to the WHOLE WORLD! You can't let ANYTHING stop you. Make new friends and travel to places you've never been and tell EVERYONE all the things I've told you!

Disciples: *(Raise their arms in victory.)* Yeah!

(Jesus leaves the stage.)

Theo: *(Reading)* Then, Theo, the STRANGEST thing happened. Jesus started to float toward heaven. I mean REALLY float toward heaven. He lifted straight off the ground and just kept GOING, until the clouds blocked him from view. And the Disciples said:

Disciples: *(Looking up to heaven)* Whoa, dude.

(Angels enter from stage right.)

Theo: *(Reading)* They were AMAZED. When they looked around they saw two men in dazzling white robes. The Angels said:

Angels: What are you doing looking at the sky? Jesus has gone home like he said, and just like he said, he'll be back.

Theo: *(Reading)* And the Disciples said…

Disciples: Whoa, dude.

Theo: *(Reading)* Then the ANGELS said…

Angels: So, why are you standing around HERE? You've got WORK to do.

Theo: (*Reading*) And the Disciples said…

Disciples: (*Raise their arms in victory.*) Yeah!

Theo: (*Reading*) I've got plenty more to write about. I'm going to tell you ALL the Acts of the Apostles before we're through!

To Talk About

◆ How do you think the disciples felt about their new assignment?

◆ Jesus wanted the disciples to go to their enemies, the Samaritans, with the good news of Jesus. Without naming names, have you ever had to love an enemy because Jesus wanted you to?

◆ Who is one person that you should share the good news of Jesus with? Let's pray for those people together right now.

Topical Tie-Ins: Witnessing, Ascension of Christ, Loving Enemies

Speak Up!

The Scene: a house

The Simple Setup: an open stage—no furniture needed

For Extra Impact: Give the Tongues of Fire each a length of orange or red crepe paper to hold above the heads of Peter and the Believers. You could also give the Wind sheets of poster board to wave for sound effects.

Bible Story
Pentecost

Scripture
Acts 2:1-24, 36-41

The Characters

Narrator: a friendly storyteller

Peter: a guy or a girl

John: a guy or a girl

Other Disciples: guys or girls

Tongues of Fire: kids willing to twinkle their fingers like flames above the heads of the Disciples

Crowd: kids willing to be people listening to Peter

The Skit

After you've assigned the roles of Peter and John, form children into three groups: the Other Disciples, the Crowd, and Tongues of Fire. If you have just a few children, let them play multiple roles.

As the skit begins, the stage is empty except for Peter, John, and the Disciples, at center stage. The Tongues of Fire and Crowd are off stage left.

Peter: It's been awhile since Jesus went back to heaven, but he told us to wait here in Jerusalem. So I guess that's what we keep doing, right?

John: Makes sense to ME. Jesus said something about God sending us a gift. I hope it's a new DONKEY—I could really USE a new donkey.

Peter: I don't know what the gift is, but I'm pretty sure it's NOT a donkey.

John: YOU don't know. It COULD be a donkey!

Peter: Trust me, there's NO WAY he meant…

Start the "Pentecost" track on *The Humongous Book of Bible Skits for Children's Ministry* **CD (track 49). Set your CD on "repeat" so the track repeats.**

John: Hey—what's that sound?

Peter: Whatever it is, I don't think it's a DONKEY.

John: I hear it too! It sounds like a TRAIN coming toward us!

Peter: What's a TRAIN?

John: Oh, I forgot—they haven't been INVENTED yet. NEVER mind. It sounds like WIND rushing toward us! Yeah, THAT'S what it sounds like—lots of WIND! This is AMAZING!

(Tongues of Fire appear over the heads of John, Peter, and the Disciples.)

Peter: Wow! those look like TONGUES OF FLAME!

John: And there's a TONGUE OF FLAME over each of our heads! What's going ON here?

Peter: Guten tag!

John: What did you say, Peter? What language WAS that?

Peter: I THINK it was German.

John: I didn't know you could SPEAK German!

Peter: Neither did I. Wait a minute, I CAN'T speak German! Guten tag! There it goes AGAIN!

John: Hey, it's happening to ME, too! ¡Gracias!

Narrator: The Disciples all walked outside. A Crowd quickly gathered, because no matter what language the people in the crowd SPOKE, they heard words in their native tongues.

(The Crowd forms around Peter, at center stage.)

No one could figure out how it was possible for ONE disciple to be speaking and yet his words could be understood in so MANY languages! Some members of the crowd elbowed each other and pointed. They thought the Disciples must be drunk.

Peter: Listen, everyone! We are NOT drunk! The Bible said God would pour out his Holy Spirit, and that's what HAPPENED here. Don't you understand?

Narrator: The crowd apparently DIDN'T understand. Not in ANY language. So Peter explained further.

Peter: Don't you GET it? God wants you to believe in Jesus, who was crucified and who was raised from the dead. Now Jesus sits at God's right hand. Jesus is Lord and MESSIAH! God sent his Holy Spirit to us today to help you believe!

Narrator: Thousands of people in the Crowd realized that what Peter said was true. AND it explained the miracle they were seeing! They called out:

Crowd: What should we do?

Narrator: Peter had an answer.

Peter: Each of you needs to turn AWAY from your sins and BELIEVE in Jesus.

Narrator: What an amazing day! The crowd listened, nodding their heads and clapping their hands. And that day about 3,000 people believed in Jesus!

 ## To Talk About

◆ **Seeing the power of the Holy Spirit helped lots of people believe in Jesus that day. How can the Holy Spirit help you believe in Jesus?**

◆ **Some people laughed at the disciples, but Peter spoke boldly of his faith. What can you do if someone laughs at you for being a Christian?**

◆ **By telling others about his faith, Peter helped 3,000 believe in Jesus on the day of Pentecost. What can you do this week to help someone believe in Jesus?**

Topical Tie-Ins: Holy Spirit, Faith, Witnessing

The Stoning of Stephen

Bible Story
Stoning of Stephen

Scripture
Acts 6:8–8:1

The Scene: Jerusalem, 30 A.D.

The Simple Setup: You'll need no furniture on stage; keep the stage open so it's easy for the crowd to move around.

For Extra Impact: Since we're dealing with the violence of stoning, pantomiming is the best way to go. If you want to add a little realism, use paper wads for stones.

The Characters

Narrator: a nice storyteller
Freedman 1: a guy
Freedman 2: a guy

Sanhedrin: the rest of the class
Stephen: a guy

The Skit

After assigning the roles of Freedman 1, Freedman 2, and Stephen, assign the rest of the children to the role of the Sanhedrin.

As the skit begins, the Sanhedrin are stage left. They'll rush to center stage during the stoning. Freedman 1 and Freedman 2 are with the Sanhedrin. Stephen is center stage.

Narrator: There was once a good man named Stephen who loved the Lord with all of his heart, mind, and soul. But as we'll soon learn, just because you do the right THINGS doesn't mean that the world always treats you in the right WAY.

Freedman 1: *(Walking back and forth angrily)* That STEPHEN thinks he's so good. He thinks he's so SMART.

Freedman 2: *(Standing still, but watching the first guy)* But he IS smart.

Freedman 1: *(Still walking)* I know, but that doesn't mean that I have to LIKE it. He thinks he does so many good things.

Freedman 2: But he DOES do a lot of good things. He even does miracles and wonders. Besides, he helps feed all those poor WIDOW ladies.

Freedman 1: I know! I know! But that doesn't mean I have to LIKE it. And you know what ELSE he does? He tells people about JESUS!

Freedman 2: OK…now THAT could be a problem!

Freedman 1: You BET it is! We put JESUS to death because he said he was God's Son, and now this Stephen is saying the SAME THING! We've got to tell the SANHEDRIN about this!

(Freedman 1 and 2 join the Sanhedrin. They all huddle up like they're talking about something.)

Narrator: The Sanhedrin was like Israel's supreme court. There were 71 men on the court, and they met to talk when someone did something really bad…like talk about JESUS. That's because the Sanhedrin didn't believe Jesus was God's Son. The Freedmen went and got Stephen, and brought him before the Sanhedrin.

(Stephen walks to center stage and faces the Sanhedrin.)

Stephen: You wanted to see me?

Narrator: The charge against Stephen was blasphemy—which meant he was saying untrue things about God. Stephen was saying Jesus was God's Son.

Freedman 1: *(Moves to center stage where he points at Stephen.)* I heard this man say that Jesus of Nazareth will DESTROY this place. AND he said bad things about Moses!

Sanhedrin: *(Looking at each other)* These are SERIOUS charges. Are they TRUE?

Stephen: I know God has always been with our people. God asked Abraham to leave his country and go to a new land.

Sanhedrin: *(Folding their arms and nodding their heads)* That's true. So far, so good.

Stephen: So Abraham went where God showed him, and God told Abraham that his children would inherit the land. The only problem was that Abraham was an old man who didn't have any kids.

Sanhedrin: *(Looking at each other with pride)* Still true.

Stephen: But Abraham still believed God. Then along came Joseph who went to Egypt.

Sanhedrin: Still true. But what about JESUS?

Stephen: After Joseph died, along came a king who made our people slaves.

Sanhedrin: *(Dropping their heads)* Sad…but still true.

Stephen: Then came Moses. He knew he was one of us, but God let him be raised in Pharaoh's house. Moses was the one who finally led our people out of that awful place.

Sanhedrin: *(Raising their arms in victory)* That's true! Woo-hoo!

Stephen: Moses took notes from God and gave us the commandments.

Sanhedrin: *(Give each other high fives with both hands over their heads.)* That's true, too! Give me a high ten!

Stephen: But our people didn't obey Moses or God's commandments. That caused a HUGE problem.

Sanhedrin: *(Shaking their heads)* We don't LIKE that part, but it's true!

Stephen: The people made an idol, and God was upset about it.

Sanhedrin: *(Shaking their heads)* Still true—but about this JESUS thing...

Stephen: God kept his promise and Abraham's people finally found a home in the Promised Land.

Sanhedrin: True—we're here NOW.

Stephen: But our people kept not following God. That's still true. You guys are always pushing God to the limit to see how far he'll go.

Sanhedrin: *(Starting to get angry)* Hey! WAIT a minute!

Stephen: You guys are just like your fathers. You're pushing God's patience right this MINUTE.

Sanhedrin: *(Getting angry)* Watch your step!

Stephen: Your forefathers hurt every single person God sent to talk to you. You even killed the ones who told you about Jesus' coming!

Sanhedrin: *(Raising their hands in anger)* Be QUIET!

Stephen: Then you even killed the Righteous One himself! Won't you guys ever LEARN?

Narrator: That was all the Sanhedrin could handle. They covered their EARS so they couldn't hear, and they opened their MOUTHS and let out a nastiest roar! They were TOTALLY angry!

Sanhedrin: Stephen is GUILTY! He says Jesus is GOD'S SON! STONE him!

Start the "Stoning of Stephen" track on *The Humongous Book of Bible Skits for Children's Ministry* **CD (track 50). Set your CD player on "repeat" so the track repeats.**

Narrator: And that's what they did. The Sanhedrin took Stephen outside Jerusalem, and they picked up some rocks. They threw rocks at Stephen as hard as they COULD. Stephen looked up toward heaven.

Stephen: I can see Jesus, and he's standing up to meet me.

Sanhedrin: *(Keep throwing.)* Get him! Get him! Somebody hand me another ROCK!

Stephen: Father, don't hold a grudge against these guys. They really don't understand what's going on. *(Stephen then dies.)*

Narrator: And then Stephen died. The Sanhedrin left that day not knowing what they'd done. They knew that they'd killed STEPHEN, but they DIDN'T know that he'd been telling the TRUTH. And they DIDN'T know the man who was holding their coats was Saul, who would become the greatest MISSIONARY the world had ever seen!

To Talk About

◆ How did Stephen keep such a great attitude even though the Sanhedrin was abusing him?

◆ Have you ever been in a situation where you were doing the right thing but the right thing wasn't being done to you?

◆ Stephen forgave the men who were killing him. Without naming names, are there some people who you should forgive for something they've done or are doing?

Topical Tie-Ins: Persecution, Witnessing, Forgiveness

Saul Gets a Talkin' To

Bible Story
Saul's Conversion

Scripture
Acts 9:1-19

The Scene: the road to Damascus, Judas' house

The Simple Setup: No furniture is necessary. Place one child with a flashlight offstage to shine on Saul during the first scene.

For Extra Impact: Turn off the lights when Saul is blinded, and put a blindfold on Saul.

The Characters

Narrator: a friendly storyteller
Saul: a boy
Voice of Jesus: a boy

People Traveling With Saul: kids who will be present for Saul's conversion
Ananias: a boy

The Skit

After you've assigned the roles of Saul, Ananias, and the Voice of Jesus, ask the rest of your children to be People Traveling With Saul.

As the skit begins, Saul and the People Traveling With Saul will be slowly walking from stage left to stage right. The Voice of Jesus will be offstage, as will the Narrator.

Start the "Saul's Conversion" track on *The Humongous Book of Bible Skits for Children's Ministry* CD (track 51). Set your CD player on "repeat" so the track repeats.

Narrator: As our story begins, Saul and his buddies are walking on a road toward the city of Damascus.

Saul: Boy, it's HOT out here! It feels like we've been walking for DAYS.

People: *(Whining)* Are we THERE yet? I'm HUNGRY! I'm TIRED!

Saul: I think we'll be there soon. And when we DO get to Damascus, these Christian folks had better watch OUT, because they're going to JAIL!

Narrator: Suddenly, a bright light from heaven shone on Saul.

(A flashlight from offstage shines on Saul. People Traveling With Saul fall on the ground, blinded by the light.)

Voice of Jesus: *(Offstage)* Saul, Saul, why do you persecute me?

(Saul also falls to his knees.)

Saul: OW! My EYES! I can't see! Who is it talking to me? Who ARE you, Lord?

Voice of Jesus: I am Jesus, who YOU have been persecuting. Now get up and go into the city, and you'll be told what to do.

Narrator: Then the light went away.

(Turn off the flashlight.)

People: *(Standing up slowly and brushing themselves off)* What WAS that?

Narrator: The people thought it might have been lightning, or perhaps some OTHER natural event. They noticed that Saul looked strange. He rubbed his eyes, and then held his hand in front of his eyes. He rubbed his eyes again.

Saul: *(Doesn't speak right away; looks shaken.)* I'm still alive…*(Rises and staggers.)* But I can't SEE! I'm BLIND! Which way is Damascus? I have to go to the city!

(Saul starts walking the wrong way. The People Traveling With Saul turn him around to go in the right direction. Everyone walks off stage right.)

Stop playing track 51.

Narrator: Saul was blind for three days. He didn't eat or drink anything. And while Saul was recovering, there was a man named Ananias who was going about his daily life without a care in the world.

(Ananias comes to center stage. Saul walks just onstage, stage right.)

Narrator: Ananias was a Christian. One morning he was praying and he heard a message from Jesus.

Voice of Jesus: Hey, Ananias! I have a special ASSIGNMENT for you. Have you heard of a man named Saul?

Ananias: That guy who makes fun of you and puts Christians in jail? PLEASE don't make me talk to him! He'd probably arrest me or cut my HEAD off or something!

Voice of Jesus: Don't worry. Saul and I had a little CHAT. He won't be hurting Christians anymore. But I need you to go talk to Saul. He's expecting you. I've chosen him to be a great Christian leader.

Ananias: Saul? A Christian? A Christian LEADER? Well, if you say so…I'll go to the house where he's staying.

(Ananias walks over to Saul.)

Saul: Hello?

Ananias: Hi, Saul. Jesus told me to stop by. I'm a Christian, and I heard you don't hurt us anymore. I'm HOPING I heard that right!

Saul: That's true, friend. I'm ashamed of how I treated the Lord's people.

Ananias: Boy, THAT'S a relief! Say, would you like some help with your sight?

Saul: What can YOU do?

Ananias: Saul, the Lord Jesus has sent me so that you can see again and be filled with the Holy Spirit. I'm going to put my hands on your shoulders. Ready?

Saul: Ready.

(Ananias puts his hands on Saul's shoulders.)

Saul: I…I can see! I'm HEALED!

Ananias: Welcome to the family, brother Saul!

To Talk About

◆ Jesus got Saul's attention in a big way—Saul was blind for three days. What does Jesus do to get your attention?

◆ Why do you think Jesus chose Saul to be a Christian leader?

◆ At first Ananias was afraid to talk to Saul. Then Jesus gave Ananias courage to do what Jesus asked. Tell about a time you were nervous and Jesus gave you courage.

Topical Tie-Ins: Becoming a Christian, Forgiveness, Sin, Courage

Sleepwalking

The Scene: the prison and surrounding neighborhood
The Simple Setup: Make simple prison bars by hanging crepe paper "prison bars" from the ceiling.
For Extra Impact: For an extra-cool prison, convert a large appliance box into a backdrop for the prison walls. Consider allowing the children to use tempera paint and sponges to blot "stones" on the prison walls.

Bible Story
Peter's Prison Escape

Scripture
Acts 12:1-19

The Characters

Colorado Riviera, Investigative Reporter: a friendly reader, can be a boy or a girl
Herod: a boy, Herod has a *mean* streak
Peter: a boy or girl

Angel: a boy or a girl
Church Members: children willing to act as though in prayer
Prison Guards: two children

The Skit

After you've assigned the roles of Colorado Riviera, Herod, Peter, Angel, and Prison Guards, have the rest of the children play the part of Church Members. If you have just a few children, let children play both Church Members and Prison Guards.

Build the prison at stage left. The scene opens with Herod standing in front of the prison, the Church Members and Peter standing stage right. Colorado Riviera is on all fours at one corner of the stage area.

Start the "Peter's Prison Escape" track on *The Humongous Book of Bible Skits for Children's Ministry* CD (track 52). Set your CD player on "repeat" so the track repeats.

Colorado Riviera: This is Colorado Riviera, Investigative Reporter. I'm covering what is the most DANGEROUS story I've covered since last week when I broke the news that two-hump camels tend to roll over during highway driving. Any-hoo, I'm now undercover, pretending to be a donkey, and I'm watching an underground movement that's growing steadily. It's called "The Church," and every time I look, people in the church are PRAYING. Look—they're doing it AGAIN—PRAYING! It wasn't long ago that the church's FOUNDER, Jesus, was CRUCIFIED. But thousands of people are following Jesus anyway. Look! There they go AGAIN! PRAYING!

Now King Herod is walking toward me. WHAT an opportunity for an exclusive interview! King Herod! King Herod! A moment of your time, please!

Herod: Why, a talking DONKEY! THIS is something you don't see every day!

Colorado Riviera: King, why are you so MEAN to the Christians—the people in the church?

Herod: That's easy. Popularity! The people I rule are happy when I clamp down on Jesus' followers. When I had Jesus' brother, James, put to death, my popularity rose 14 percent!

Colorado Riviera: It seems you're targeting church leaders, King. I'm thinking it's a good thing you don't know that PETER is in town!

Herod: What? PETER is here?

Colorado Riviera: Oops…that was supposed to be a SECRET!

Herod: THANKS, Donkey! If I could capture and kill PETER, think how much the Jewish leaders would applaud me THEN. My ratings would go up 50 percent!

Colorado Riviera: Look, if you could just forget I SAID anything…

Herod: Guards! Go arrest Peter!

Guards: Yes, sir!

(Guards go to where Church Members are praying and grab Peter.)

Colorado Riviera: This is AWFUL! The Guards grabbed Peter and tossed him in PRISON!

Herod: This is PERFECT! Guards, handcuff yourselves to Peter's wrists! *(Pause.)* Good. Now keep an eye on Peter—he MUST die!

Colorado Riviera: This is a DISASTER! I, Colorado Riviera, have made a HUGE mistake! I've betrayed a source! What will this do to my REPUTATION?

Herod: You're a talking donkey. I wouldn't think your reputation could get much LOWER.

Colorado Riviera: Wait—there's STILL hope! Maybe the CHURCH MEMBERS will rise up and attack the prison! Maybe they'll overpower the Guards and RESCUE Peter! I'll just sneak over there and take a LOOK. What? They're just PRAYING! At a time they SHOULD be organizing RESCUE TEAMS, they've got their eyes closed and HEADS bowed! I may have to rescue Peter MYSELF! I'll just sneak a peek into the window of the prison…Nope—nothing I can do. Peter is sleeping, and the Guards are on duty. What's this? An ANGEL has appeared in front of Peter! Peter's shackles have FALLEN OFF!

Angel: Hey sleepyhead. Do you want to escape or NOT? Wake up! I've come to RESCUE you.

Peter: Five more minutes, Mommy, just five more minutes. THEN I'll get up and go to school.

Angel: We aren't GOING to school. I'm getting you out of this PRISON.

Peter: Just five more minutes…

Angel: Hurry UP. Get your sandals on, pull on your cloak—we're leaving NOW!

Colorado Riviera: Peter isn't fully awake, but at least he's dressed. The Angel is leading sleepy Peter out of the prison.

Peter: Angel, have you ever had that dream where you were standing in front of the school and you realized that you were wearing nothing but your underwear? I HATE that dream.

Angel: Can't say I have, Peter.

Peter: And then I had this dream that I was in PRISON, and the Church Members were praying for me, and an ANGEL showed up.

Colorado Riviera: The Angel is leading Peter past all the Guards. Somehow the Guards don't even SEE Peter! Now we're approaching the iron gates of the city. There's no WAY to get past them. But…LOOK! The doors have swung open, and they're passing though. And now Peter is waking up.

Peter: What…what HAPPENED? I had this DREAM that an ANGEL rescued me. The Angel made Guards fall asleep…and there was this iron door, and I'm free. FREE! FREE! It WASN'T a dream. God SAVED me!

Colorado Riviera: Peter is running to where the Church Members are praying. They're CELEBRATING! Now they're thanking God for hearing their prayers! This is Colorado Riviera, signing off! With…

Herod: Hey, Donkey.

Colorado Riviera: Um…King Herod! What are YOU doing out at this hour?

Herod: Since we've got Peter locked down tight, I thought I'd find YOU.

Colorado Riviera: But WHY?

Herod: You're kidding, right? A talking donkey? You're worth a FORTUNE! I'm sticking you in the royal ZOO!

 ## To Talk About

◆ Herod was willing to hurt Christians to be popular with the people he ruled. Have you ever been tempted to do wrong things so others would like you? How did you handle that temptation?

◆ How important do you think the church's prayers were in Peter's rescue? Do you think God would have sent the angel if the church *hadn't* prayed? Why or why not?

◆ How do you think this whole experience changed Peter's life? What do you think his attitude toward prayer was after that night?

Topical Tie-Ins: Prayer, God's Protection, Popularity

Indexes

Bible Characters Index

Topical Index

CD Tracks

You'll find these 52 tracks of sound effects on *The Humongous Book of Bible Skits for Children's Ministry* CD!

1. Adam and Eve
2. Cain and Abel
3. Noah
4. Tower of Babel
5. Joseph and His Brothers
6. Joseph Interprets Pharaoh's Dreams
7. Birth of Moses
8. Moses and the Burning Bush
9. Crossing the Red Sea
10. The Ten Commandments Given and Received
11. The Golden Calf
12. Spies in Canaan
13. Gideon and the Midianites
14. Ruth
15. Samuel Anoints David
16. David and Goliath
17. David and Jonathan
18. Solomon's Wisdom
19. Elijah and the Prophets of Baal
20. Naaman Healed of Leprosy
21. Shadrach, Meshach, and Abednego
22. Daniel and the Lions' Den
23. Jonah Flees From God
24. Birth of Jesus
25. Jesus at the Temple
26. Jesus Calls the First Disciples
27. Water Into Wine
28. Jesus Heals a Paralyzed Man
29. Jesus Walks on the Water
30. Jesus Feeds 5,000
31. 10 Healed of Leprosy
32. Lazarus Raised From the Dead
33. Wise and Foolish Builders
34. Widow's Offering
35. Mary and Martha
36. Zacchaeus
37. Parable of the Sower
38. Parable of the Good Samaritan
39. Parable of the Prodigal Son
40. The Triumphant Entry
41. Jesus Washes the Disciples' Feet
42. The Last Supper
43. Jesus Arrested
44. Jesus Resurrected
45. Jesus Appears to Mary
46. Walk to Emmaus
47. Jesus Appears to Thomas
48. Jesus Taken to Heaven
49. Pentecost
50. Stoning of Stephen
51. Saul's Conversion
52. Peter's Prison Escape